Retail Advertising
A Management Approach

Richard J. Gentile

Lebhar-Friedman Books
Chain Store Publishing Corp.
A Subsidiary of Lebhar-Friedman, Inc., New York

Contents

Part II

Part III

Part I

1

The Function of Advertising in the Retail Organization

If all things were perfect for the retailer—the times, sources of supply, sales help, and all the other basics of retailing, he still would be challenged by a multitude of daily problems which would keep him busy every day of the week. Consistent problems and challenges are the nature of the retail business.

Still, with all the problems and changes that today's economy has brought, the basic purpose of retailing is the same as in centuries past—to move goods to and through the store for profit. The test of the good merchant, therefore, is in how well he anticipates the modern consumer's needs. *Retail advertising is merely the retailer's announcement or expression of his anticipation of these needs.* The basic advertising premise is a very simple one: If a department of goods is worth carrying, it is worth advertising.

Effective retail advertising should accomplish the following:

- Increase sales transactions and volume
- Increase inventory turns
- Help meet predetermined sales goals (the budget)

The success or failure of the retailer in achieving these three objectives will be largely determined by the accuracy of his prediction of consumer needs, i.e. his merchandising decisions.

To increase turns and realize higher sales volume, a retailer must present an adequate item-mix and reflect that mix in effective advertising and promotion. He judges his success or failure by one very important yardstick—the cash register. A cash register yardstick does not imply that all items must produce a designated amount of sales. However, it does mean that the line of goods or the department must compare favorably to the total store performance and expected total sales budgets.

In retailing, some items generate traffic (people) while others generate profit or a large dollar volume or both. The retailer must understand this when he considers merchandise for his item-mix. Thus, advertising to the retailer is considerably more than just corporate image or layout, art work, and copy. All of these, of course, are important, but when there is a lack of basic merchandising sense, a lack of understanding of what really satisfies the consumer's wants and needs, the retailer will be hard pressed to keep producing effective ads.

THE DIFFERENCE BETWEEN ADVERTISING AND SALES PROMOTION

During any particular period, the retailer may wish to accelerate the movement of goods. He does this with sales promotion which supplements his advertising, display, and personal selling programs.

For example, imagine a retailer who, at first signs of warm weather, announces that his store will feature Brand "X" sport shirts in a wide range of colors and sizes. Our retailer has bought heavily and can afford to sell the shirts at ten percent off the regular price for a two-day selling period. In addition, a special display has been constructed and a 50-cent incentive offered to all employees in the department for each shirt sold.

In this instance, only the announcement of the sale was an advertising expenditure. The ten percent markdown on each shirt sold, the cost of the special display, and the 50-cent incentive to employees were sales promotion expenditures.

The astute retailer who has learned by hard experience at no time allows sales promotion expenses to be charged to the advertising account. Every department or line of goods carried must have its advertising dollars protected for the primary use of announcement of anticipated consumer needs. Dissipation of advertising dollars by sales promotion charge-backs reduces the frequency and impact of announcements of special sales.

THE MARRIAGE OF RETAIL ADVERTISING AND MERCHANDISING

The retailer is, or should be, a merchant. He merchandises his space, whether it be floor space or newspaper advertising space, with a presentation of the right items, at the right time, in the right quantities, at the right price.

Merchandising must enter into the advertising function from the very inception. Advertising does not begin with copy information and end with the release of the completed advertisement to media. The retail advertising function begins with the release of an approved six or 12-month sales budget for each department or, for the smaller store, for each line of goods. From this point, advertising strategies can be developed.

It is true that advertising announces the retailer's anticipations of consumer needs, but these announcements are merely presentations of some strategically selected and placed items. Unfortunately, the majority of retailers do not approach advertising in this way. They do not see it as the proper extension of the merchandising function.

To make the union of merchandising and advertising work properly, merchandising people also must learn to look at advertising in its true light. If problem items or overstocks are consistently selected for advertising instead of the proven items, it should eventually become obvious to the buyer or department manager that he is not using his advertising dollars to the best advantage. He should stop spending good dollars to advertise items the consumer has already said she does not want.

Successful retail advertising is a presentation of a timely and deliberate mix of various ad types and item types. Some items produce large unit sales, others produce dollar volume while others introduce a great deal of both into the store. Some items are highly promotional while others are highly seasonal and still others are basics the consumer wants regardless of price or time of the year. Similarly, in every advertisement, each piece of merchandise has its proper place as a feature, secondary feature (sub-feature), or a traffic-building item. In addition, each item falls within a certain price range—low end, middle, or top. It is the proper "mix" of both the merchandise and advertising strategy that yields advertising success.

YARDSTICKS FOR MANAGEMENT

All retail operating and merchandising expenditures, including ending inventories, advertising, display, and sales promotion are planned for in advance to departmental six-month or yearly sales budgets (to be discussed in more detail in later chapters). For meaningful control, the retailer should establish specific yardsticks to measure progress towards these budgeted sales goals. It is imperative to compare actual performances to sales budget expectations, department by department and line by line—even item by item if it is necessary.

Because advertising is so important to overall store and chain performance, it must be scrutinized before, during, and after the fact. Two reports any retailer can develop for purposes of advertising comparisons are a monthly advertising report and a monthly merchandise performance comparison. With these two reports, management can immediately determine causes of known effects. The reports afford management the opportunity to decipher fact from intuition, quickly and efficiently.

The monthly merchandise performance comparison lists, by department, budgeted sales, actual sales, percentage of increase or decrease over the previous year, departmental receipt of goods, selling value and markup, permanent markdowns taken during the month, promotional markdowns taken, closing inventory (budgeted and actual), sales returns, budgeted sales for the next two months, and other items such as on-order dollars and budgets.

Used to complement the merchandise performance report, the advertising report lists, also departmentally, the month's net sales, net newspaper dollar advertising expenditures, circular (pre-prints) expenditures, television and radio expenditures, and the percentage of these expenditures to net sales. The net sales and advertising expenditures with their percentages also are listed for the year to date. The report should also list all other miscellaneous advertising charges and credits for the month and year to date. With both the monthly advertising report and the merchandise performance comparison, management has all the figures required to determine the cause and corrective action for lagging sales.

The retailer should fully understand and keep in mind the fact that all retail expenses, merchandise purchases, and advertising expenditures are based on estimated sales. When budgeted sales are missed, that is the moment problems begin. That is the time to pay particular attention to the monthly advertising and merchandising reports.

Imagine a store with 40 departments. For the first five months of the year, the store had a ten percent sales decrease over the comparable period the year before. This would not be a serious problem had the store been budgeted for a ten percent decrease because operating and advertising budgets would have been pared down proportionately. But for the sake of this illustration, let us say that, instead, the store was budgeted for a three percent sales increase.

The retailer (manager) not only missed his budgeted three percent increase, but he also realized a serious sales decrease from the previous year. Missed sales budgets result in inventory overages and lead to more markdowns, more old merchandise, slower turns, and possibly a reduction in ordering new goods which in turn leads to out-of-stocks of basic items. Because of the serious implications of a missed budget, cause must be determined as quickly as possible.

At the time the retailer finalized his budgeted sales, he took into consideration his local marketing factors, sales trends, and economy indicators. It is true that the economy might have changed in a year. However, he cannot blame his ten percent sales decrease on the economy until he reviews his monthly advertising and merchandising reports.

A quick review of the two reports tells our retailer that of his 40 departments, the ten percent decrease was restricted to only ten of them. Of the ten, three departments represented 70 percent of the total dollar decrease. Comparing the year's advertising report to last year's, of the three departments, one had 50 percent less advertising than last year. The second department of the three had markup on receipts that far exceeded the norm for the chain. The third department had sales returns way above normal and promotional markdowns that far exceeded budget.

After studying the two reports, the manager realized that a cut in advertising, over-pricing, and over-selling the wrong merchandise were at the root of the problem. Without disturbing or penalizing his other 37 departments, our retailer was able to take immediate action to correct the difficulties in the specific problem departments.

THE ADVERTISING FUNCTION, CENTRALIZED AND DECENTRALIZED

For the retailer with more than one store in multiple markets, the advertising function will be set up in one of two systems, centralized or decentralized.

A centralized advertising program is one in which the advertising budget, the ad schedule, ad preparation, and the merchandising of ad space are all initiated and finalized by the home office or a central region or zone office. Each store must run the ads offered by the central advertising department "as is" on the day scheduled by the central office. Decentralized advertising allows stores themselves to devise their own advertising schedules, choosing the ads from those offered by the chain advertising department.

Centralized advertising usually operates at a lower advertising ratio to sales than does decentralized advertising. It also tends to yield fewer sales per square foot of selling space and always presents the danger of contributing to an unbalanced merchandise stock condition in some stores.

Decentralization of a chain's advertising function involves considerably more than the delegation of responsibility and authority. A sophisticated decentralized advertising function, in truth, is the driving force behind an effective centralized buying program. The central buying department, in addition to supplying each store with basics for its departments, offers special promotional items to the local stores. In a sense, the buying department must "sell" its merchandise selections to the local stores which, in a decentralized system, can decide whether or not to feature particular merchandise for promotion. Each store orders according to the needs of its own clientele. The store is free to "merchandise" item by item in departments, featuring those items that will do best in that particular store.

With a centralized advertising program, the buying department must spread all bought goods out to all stores. There is generally considerable consultation with the individual stores, but the final decision of what will be promoted in the store is the buyer's. The advertising organization discussed throughout most of this book is a decentralized one.

2

Advertising Department Organization

The main point for initiation, control, promotion, and enforcement of advertising is the corporate or headquarter advertising department. This department is designated by many names, depending on the company—retail sales department, marketing sales department, central advertising, or several other titles. Whatever it is called, the corporate retail advertising department is to the store what the rifle is to the bullet. It creates the power source and channels activities to hit the target—budgeted sales.

THE HEADQUARTER ADVERTISING DEPARTMENT ORGANIZATION

The advertising department has a double responsibility. It must prepare the advertisements and promotional materials for stores in the field plus serve as communicator and central control center for corporate planning.

Retail advertising, as explained in this book, relates specifi-

A CORPORATE RETAIL SALES DEPARTMENT BASE

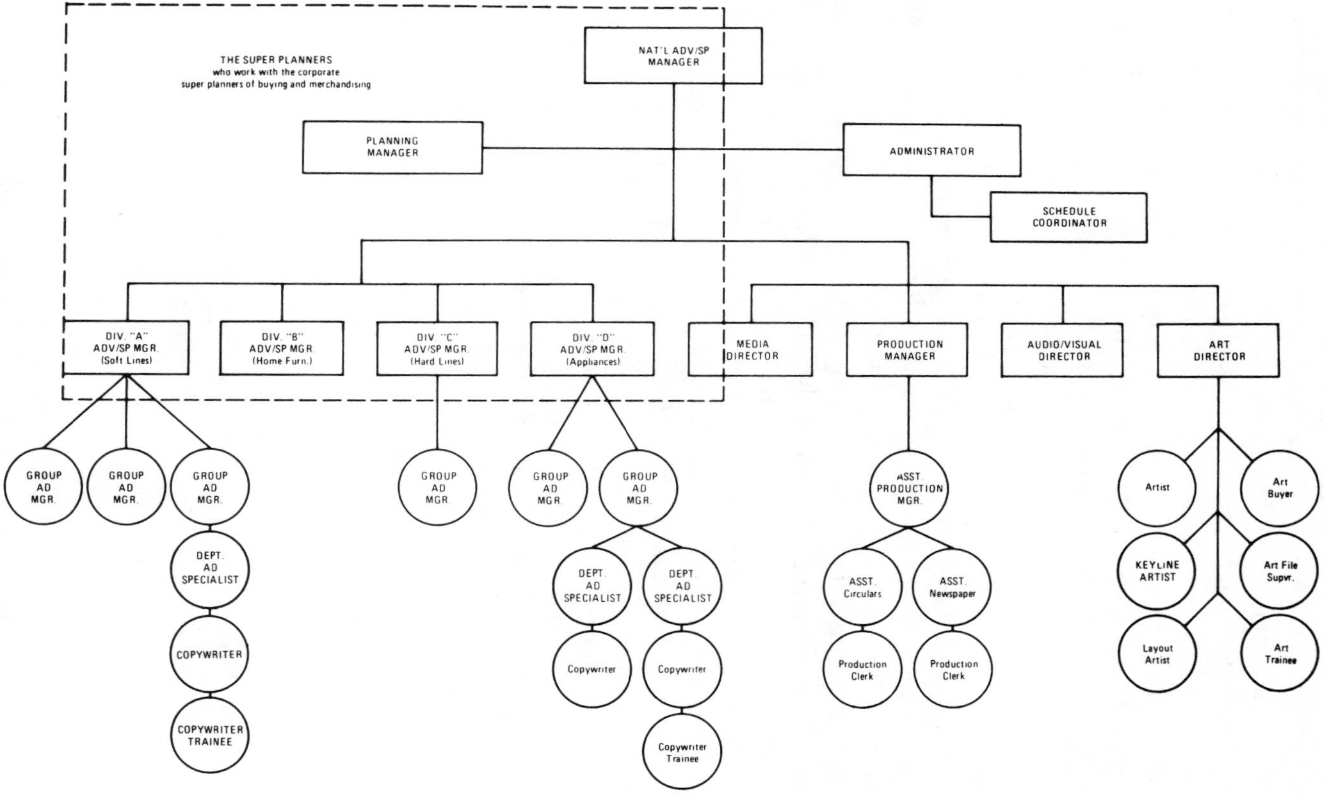

THE SUPER PLANNERS
who work with the corporate
super planners of buying and merchandising

NAT'L ADV/SP MANAGER

PLANNING MANAGER

ADMINISTRATOR

SCHEDULE COORDINATOR

DIV "A" ADV/SP MGR (Soft Lines)

DIV "B" ADV/SP MGR (Home Furn.)

DIV "C" ADV/SP MGR (Hard Lines)

DIV "D" ADV/SP MGR (Appliances)

MEDIA DIRECTOR

PRODUCTION MANAGER

AUDIO/VISUAL DIRECTOR

ART DIRECTOR

GROUP AD MGR

GROUP AD MGR

GROUP AD MGR

DEPT. AD SPECIALIST

COPYWRITER

COPYWRITER TRAINEE

GROUP AD MGR

GROUP AD MGR

GROUP AD MGR

DEPT AD SPECIALIST

DEPT AD SPECIALIST

Copywriter

Copywriter

Copywriter Trainee

ASST PRODUCTION MGR

ASST. Circulars

ASST. Newspaper

Production Clerk

Production Clerk

Art Buyer

Artist

Art File Supvr.

KEYLINE ARTIST

Art Trainee

Layout Artist

Figure 1

cally to the organizational chart in Figure 1. This structure supports the theory that the advertising person who works with a corporate buyer or merchandiser must know almost as much about the store's merchandise as the buyer or merchandiser does. The organizational chart shown is hypothetical; it does not contain a complete listing of all job classifications. However, it is quite functional if it is used as a base and structured to the retailer's specific needs. This organization, of course, is meant for a large company, but it can act as a prototype for almost any size chain.

Figure 1 illustrates the division of retail departments for purposes of advertising preparation. The departments are categorized into divisions, then subdivided into groups, then into single department headings. One division advertising/sales promotion manager may handle all departmental needs. As his group or department requirements grow, he may add a group advertising manager, then an advertising specialist or department manager, and, as required, copywriters. Or, he may proceed in the opposite direction, first adding copywriters and giving promotions up from that job to meet personnel needs. The larger a company the greater the need of an ad specialist for almost every department, but in most companies two or more departments would be assigned to an ad specialist. An exception would be for a very large and/or important department which would be delegated to one person.

Below are some of the advertising department's responsibilities (these will, of course, vary from company to company):

- Advertising and promotional merchandising policy
- Sales promotion communications
- Advertising communications
- Calendars of promotional events
- Headquarter advance planning schedules
- Sales promotion and advertising guides
- Pre-season advertising campaigns
- Co-operative advertising programs
- Monthly layouts of ads
- Communicating promotional items available
- Departmental and storewide sales contest reports

- Departmental consumer literature
- Spot radio and TV commercials
- Circular (pre-prints) planning and production
- Media contracts and research
- Monthly repro slicks of art work
- Special campaigns, grand openings, store relocations, closings, etc.
- Measurement of results
- Departmental consulting
- Deadline enforcement

Obviously, the corporate advertising department's job is a very big one, and the responsibility placed on it is one that directly affects corporate and store performance, for better or worse. It is not a department that should be subject to the "whims" of advertising managers, merchandise managers, or department managers. The effective retail advertising department should be run on set policies consistently supported by top management.

WHO PAYS FOR IT?

Few, if any, individual stores could afford the caliber of advertising personnel needed to take the responsibilities described above. However, if properly organized, a chain can.

Stores must pay for the monthly advertising package offered by chain headquarters, but the costs should not be taken from general corporate income which supports other non-advertising fixed expenses and payroll. Each store is charged for headquarter advertising payroll and costs of advertisment preparations. The methods by which this expense is charged vary. One way is to charge the store a fixed percentage of budgeted sales. This percentage is usually equal to three to five percent of the store's advertising budget. If the store prepared its own ads, it would cost five to seven percent or more of the advertising budget.

Some chains with many small stores impose a flat minimum charge on each store. The percent or amount charged depends on sales volume. Chain A, with $8.17 billion in annual sales, would charge a smaller percent to each store than would Chain B, with $100 million in annual sales.

The charge to the store for the monthly advertising service covers costs of the monthly promotional package and newspaper ad prodution costs. The charge does not include pre-printed circulars. These are offered to the stores at special prices. Nor do national advertising costs come out of the general monthly costs charged to each store. National advertising, most frequently in magazines and on television, is charged back to the specific stores within the market covered by each ad.

HOW ADVERTISING EFFECTIVENESS
DEPENDS ON CORPORATE STRUCTURE

Centralized or decentralized, the corporate advertising program will be largely a waste if it operates on one plan for all stores. Retail business is essentially local. Stores are different, and many sales patterns are seasonal. Store merchandise problems vary from department to department, and consumers, of course, vary by market. There must be some flexibility in the structure of every corporate advertising plan. The corporation itself must provide a structure which promotes this kind of flexibility.

Both Sears Roebuck and Montgomery Ward, two of the most successful advertisers and promoters, utilize flexible structures. Although first published in 1950, the Sears organizational charts (see Figure 2) still clearly illustrate the genius of structure for movement of goods. These charts, still used by Sears and by most large chains, are the prototype corporate structures.

In this organization prototype, the intricate details of store problems are handled as close to the problem as possible—in designated areas of responsibility. The corporate office is referred to by the stores as the home office, home base, and other names consistent with the idea that it is "headquarter base." It is here that all policy, systems, and methods are initiated, formalized, and enforced.

Within each region, there is a zone office with a departmental merchandising staff. The merchandise staff of the small store zones are there to assist the smaller stores which have less staff expertise and fewer staff members. The zone merchandiser may have one, three, or five different departments under his supervision. He checks these as a staff merchandiser of a larger store would check his departments.

Within each region are the groups or districts. Each is comprised of two or more of the chain's stores located in the same metropolitan area. Each store has a manager who reports to a general manager, often referred to as a group or metropolitan district manager. Promotional planning, advertisement production, and achieving sales to budgeted expectations are major responsibilities of the district staff.

The report-direct store is in a different category. It is usually a store large enough to support a full merchandising staff and advertising department. The store manager reports directly to the regional manager and his executive staff rather than to a zone or group. Departmental merchandising problems or special merchandising plans are communicated directly with parent or home office merchandise buyers. Sales per square foot of selling space are very high in most report-direct stores. Generally, these stores are the larger ones in the chain with experienced personnel that do not require everyday guidance of zone or group managers.

A CLOSER LOOK AT ORGANIZATION FOR INVENTORY CONTROL AND FLEXIBILITY

Keeping in mind that a chain is in business to move goods to and through the store, consider these possibilities the "delegated responsibility" structure discussed above promotes:

- The large report-direct store is a perfect outlet for clearing away over-buys and buying errors.

- The zone stores with different problems have their own nucleus for problem-solving. Goods can be shipped between stores. Any problem usually remains a zone problem, and does not become a corporate problem.

- Each district also has its own nucleus to solve its own problems.

- Each individual unit has company yardstick figures to apply to its operation for comparisons.

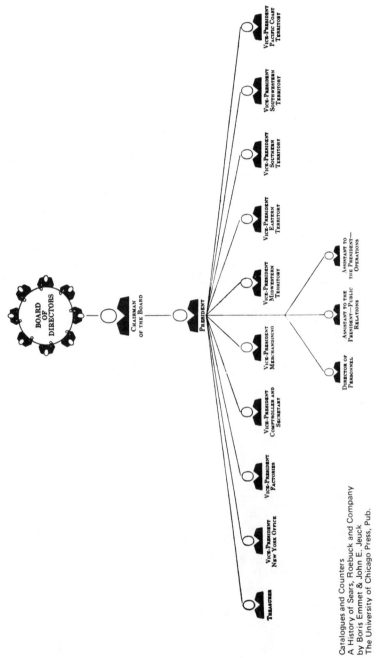

CHART I
TOP MANAGEMENT ORGANIZATION

BOARD OF DIRECTORS

CHAIRMAN OF THE BOARD

PRESIDENT

TREASURER

VICE-PRESIDENT NEW YORK OFFICE

VICE-PRESIDENT FACTORIES

VICE-PRESIDENT CONTROLLER AND SECRETARY

VICE-PRESIDENT MERCHANDISING

VICE-PRESIDENT MIDWESTERN TERRITORY

VICE-PRESIDENT EASTERN TERRITORY

VICE-PRESIDENT SOUTHERN TERRITORY

VICE-PRESIDENT SOUTHWESTERN TERRITORY

VICE-PRESIDENT PACIFIC COAST TERRITORY

DIRECTOR OF PERSONNEL

ASSISTANT TO THE PRESIDENT—PUBLIC RELATIONS

ASSISTANT TO THE PRESIDENT—OPERATIONS

Catalogues and Counters
A History of Sears, Roebuck and Company
by Boris Emmet & John E. Jeuck
The University of Chicago Press, Pub.

Figure 2

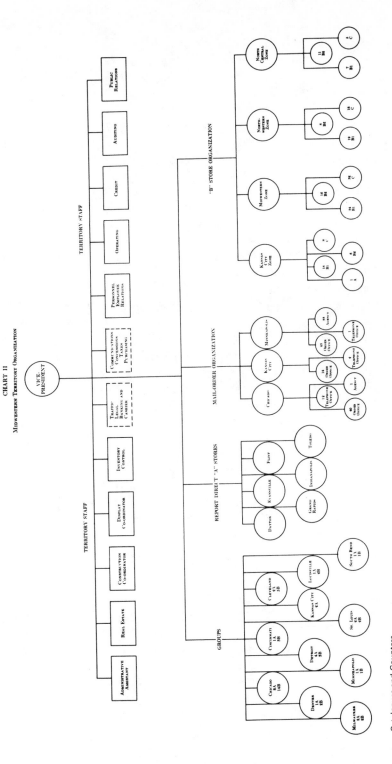

CHART II
MIDWESTERN TERRITORY ORGANIZATION

Catalogues and Counters
A History of Sears, Roebuck and Company
by Boris Emmet & John E. Jeuck
The University of Chicago Press, Pub.

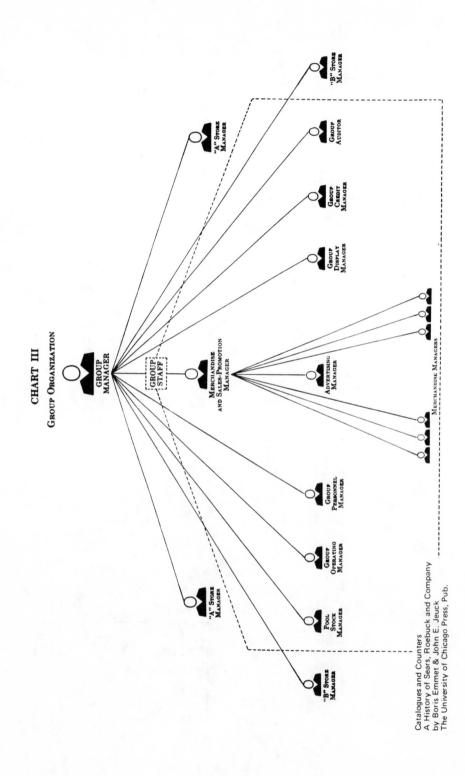

CHART III

GROUP ORGANIZATION

GROUP MANAGER

GROUP STAFF

"A" STORE MANAGER

"B" STORE MANAGER

"A" STORE MANAGER

"B" STORE MANAGER

POOL STOCK MANAGER

GROUP OPERATING MANAGER

GROUP PERSONNEL MANAGER

MERCHANDISE AND SALES-PROMOTION MANAGER

ADVERTISING MANAGER

MERCHANDISE MANAGERS

GROUP DISPLAY MANAGER

GROUP CREDIT MANAGER

GROUP AUDITOR

Catalogues and Counters
A History of Sears, Roebuck and Company
by Boris Emmet & John E. Jeuck, Pub.
The University of Chicago Press, Pub.

CHART IV

ZONE OFFICE STAFF

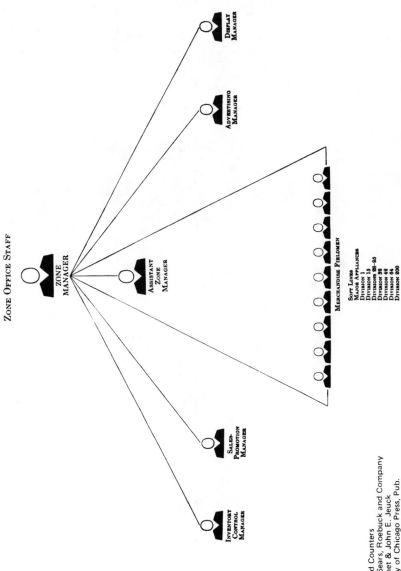

ZONE MANAGER

INVENTORY CONTROL MANAGER

SALES-PROMOTION MANAGER

ASSISTANT ZONE MANAGER

ADVERTISING MANAGER

DISPLAY MANAGER

MERCHANDISE FIELDMEN

SOFT LINES
MAJOR APPLIANCES
DIVISION 1
DIVISION 15
DIVISIONS 26-95
DIVISION 38
DIVISION 48
DIVISION 64
DIVISION 90

Catalogues and Counters
A History of Sears, Roebuck and Company
by Boris Emmet & John E. Jeuck
The University of Chicago Press, Pub.

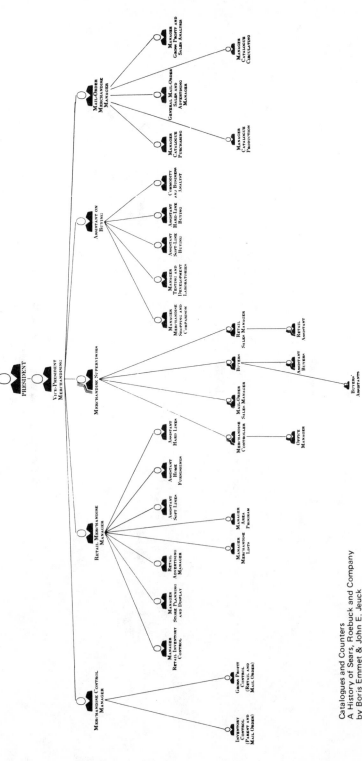

CHART V

PARENT MERCHANDISING ORGANIZATION

PRESIDENT

VICE-PRESIDENT MERCHANDISING

Merchandise Control Manager
- Inventory Control (Parent and Mail Order)
- Gross Profit Control (Retail and Mail Order)

Retail Merchandise Manager
- Manager Retail Inventory Control
- Manager Store Planning and Display
- Retail Advertising Manager
- Manager Merchandise Lists
- Manager Area Program
- Assistant Soft Lines
- Assistant Home Furnishings
- Assistant Hard Lines

Merchandise Supervisors
- Merchandise Controller
  - Office Manager
- Mail-Order Sales Manager
- Buyers
  - Assistant Buyers
  - Buyers' Assistants
- Retail Sales Manager
  - Retail Assistant

Assistant on Buying
- Manager Merchandise Shipping and Comparison
- Manager Testing and Development Laboratories
- Assistant Soft-Line Buying
- Assistant Hard-Lines Buying
- Commodity and Business Analyst

Mail-Order Merchandise Manager
- Manager Catalogue Purchasing
  - Manager Catalogue Production
- General Mail-Order Sales and Advertising Manager
  - Manager Catalogue Circulation
- Manager Gross Profit and Sales Analysis

Catalogues and Counters
A History of Sears, Roebuck and Company
by Boris Emmet & John E. Jeuck
The University of Chicago Press, Pub.

CHART VII

Independent "A" Store Organization

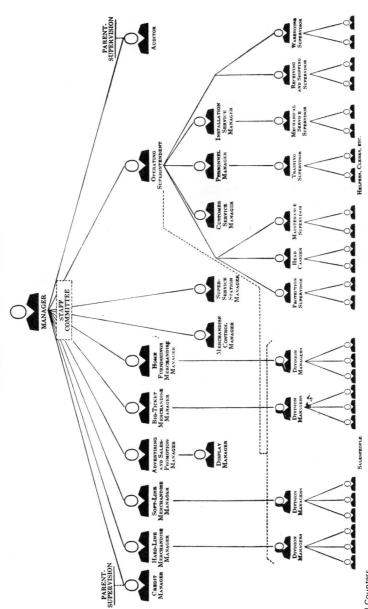

Catalogues and Counters
A History of Sears, Roebuck and Company
by Boris Emmet & John E. Jeuck
The University of Chicago Press, Pub.

The size of a particular store is determined largely by the corporate buying and merchandise departments' estimates of the store's immediate share of the market. Within the store, there will be departments of varying sizes. A very large, full line store would not have all giant departments. Basic items for each department and depth and breadth of stock are largely determined by the home office buying department. The local store can broaden or shorten its lines but first must consult with and get the approval of the main buying office.

Promotional merchandising is extremely important to the chain. The "basics," however, represent the largest percentage of goods the chain is in business to sell. These items are commonly referred to as "bread and butter" items; they carry a good markup and are the items the consumer needs and buys week in and week out. Promotional merchandising is used to supplement and accelerate these sales.

Seasonal merchandising is also an important component of chain merchandising. It involves the expansion and contraction of store merchandise departments according to local seasonal buying patterns. If a store or department does not do a satisfactory job of seasonal merchandising, a meaningful advertising program will be almost impossible. For example, in most areas snow shovels should not take up either floor space or advertising dollars in the month of April.

The advertising function is one of the responsibilities of the store manager. If sales volume permits, this responsibility might be delegated to the merchandise manager or, higher sales volume permitting, to a store advertising manager.

THE STORE ADVERTISING DEPARTMENT

Usually, when a new store is constructed, the advertising department is the last to be completed. On the blueprints, it exists as a blank area marked "advertising." Unfortunately, advertising too often gets this treatment as an unknown factor. However, when you consider that it is the largest spender of net profit dollars next to payroll, the treatment of advertising as an "unknown" seems highly questionable.

The size of the store's advertising department, if it indeed has one of its own, will, of course, be relative to the store's sales volume and advertising expenditures. For a store, advertising payroll is generally eight to 12 percent of the advertising budget. A store with a budget of $36,000 for advertising would be able to hire a part-time person to staff its advertising department, for example.

Using an hourly pay scale and applying it to the budget dollars available, one can determine the amount of advertising department man-hours that can be afforded. For example, if a retailer with a small store and an annual advertising expenditure of $9,000 (2.5 percent of annual sales volume of $360,000) applies a ten percent budgeted advertising payroll cost to the ad budget, he will have $900 available for personnel. Figuring the hourly cost for ad help is three dollars per hour (a very low figure for most areas), he will be able to afford 300 work hours. His advertising requirements will demand at least that amount of time. The breakdown probably would look like this:

Creating two six-month planning programs	38 hours (twice a year)	76
Final planning each month	5 hours (times 12)	60
Major advertising effort each month	6 hours (times 12)	72
Accounting each month	5 hours (times 12)	60
Evaluation of results each month	3 hours (times 12)	36
Total		304

Other than writing good copy and producing ads, the successful advertising department should continually work at developing a close relationship and good rapport with each department manager. The advertising department will write the advertising schedule and finalize the promotional calendar of events, but it is the department manager who must help schedule and merchandise the allocated space for his own department. The experienced advertising manager may have an idea of how he would like space merchandised, but he must suggest, not dictate, his ideas to the department manager. For any store advertising program to work, it must have the constant input of the department managers who are close to the consumer every day.

Figures 3, 4, and 5 illustrate typical floor plans for advertising departments in small, medium, and large stores. Some fixture requirements are shown in Figure 6.

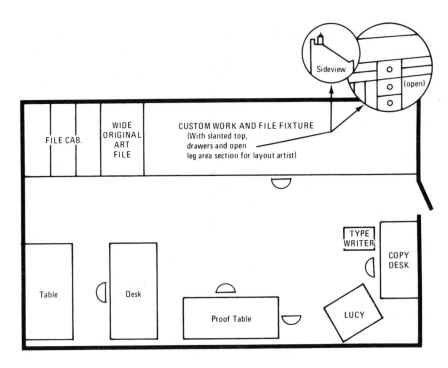

SMALL STORE ADVERTISING DEPARTMENT
2-3 PEOPLE

Figure 3

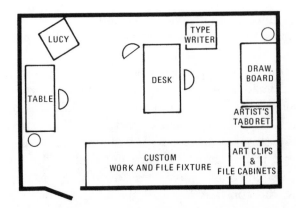

SMALL STORE ADVERTISING DEPARTMENT
1 PERSON

Figure 4

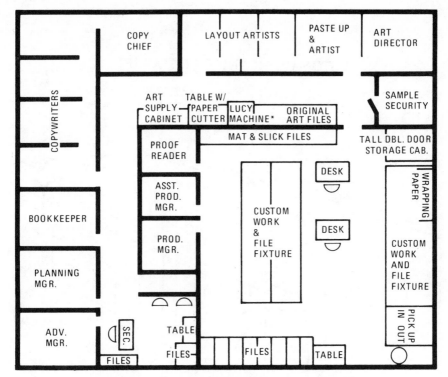

LARGE STORE ADVERTISING DEPARTMENT
14-18 PEOPLE

Notes on equipment for small stores. If the retailer is spending advertising dollars, he should have a small room set aside for that purpose. Advertising departments are very difficult to keep orderly, but when they are not, you can count on errors and wasted prep time. There must be top area to work, and there must be places to store materials. Every night before turning off the lights, the advertising room must be neat, orderly, and clean. The custom work and file fixture will help accomplish this seemingly simple but actually difficult task. For the retailer who can afford the expenditure, it will be worth the effort and price.

THE LUCY MACHINE: This machine is for the store that wishes to prepare ads from existing art. A feature item can be blown up on layout from the smallest clip. Your layout specifications will be accurate for ordering of print. It is a professional tool that pays its way by giving the layout artist the opportunity to create from what he has on hand. Cost for the "Lucy" is about $300. Used ones, if you are lucky, can be picked up for $50 to $100. They can be ordered from commercial artist stores.

TABLES: Tables are often used by the advertising department, in specific places for specific purposes. One usage is to have a table for nothing, other than for checking proofs. When there is no proof, the table is bare. The department managers like this system, and it seems to relieve pressure considerably. They always know where the proof is.

Figure 5

CUSTOM WORK AND FILE FIXTURE

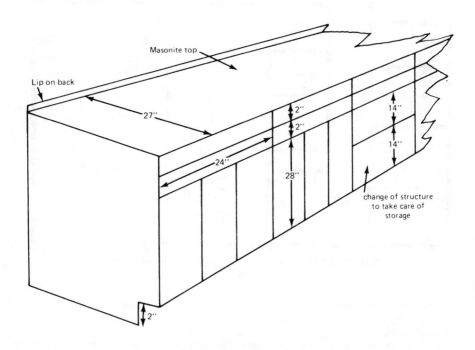

For the small store or large, one of the most useful fixtures to be found in an advertising department is custom made, of plywood construction. Its advantages are complete utilization of available space, providing sufficient work top area and, at the same time, storage space.

Figure 6

If part of a chain, the store advertising manager or the store manager will greatly depend on the package from "home;" the company monthly promotion and advertising package, prepared and mailed by the headquarter advertising department. Local store promotion planning is completely under the influence of this package.

A typical package, usually shipped under one cover, will consist of the following:

- Suggested ad layouts
- Departmental art reproduction slick service
- Contest and/or co-op advertising wrap ups
- Monthly sales and advertising comments covering all departments
- Promotional items available to stores
- Samples of pre-printed circulars available

It is important, whatever materials a headquarter office may send, that there be organization within the local store advertising department for its usage and storage. The monthly promotion and advertising package will be discussed at length later in the book.

ORGANIZATION OF STORE ADVERTISING DEPARTMENT

Because store volumes vary so much, it would be difficult to present two or three organizational suggestions that would serve the needs of all retailers. Therefore, one prototype organization chart for a store advertising department is presented, in Figure 7.

The departmental organization illustrated shows the proper flow of information needed to write the advertising copy. The most difficult and crucial stage in producing an ad is the very beginning. If copy information is not complete and accurate, the possibility of later errors is increased, and considerable time will be wasted when the error is discovered and corrected.

If there is more than one copywriter, each can develop ex-

STORE ADVERTISING DEPARTMENT ORGANIZATION

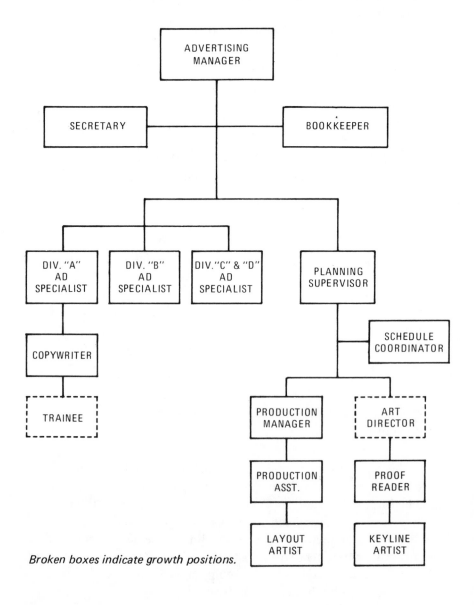

Broken boxes indicate growth positions.

Figure 7

pertise in specific departments. Each will have the resource materials and the knowledge needed to write sales-producing ads for their respective departments. Specifics of writing copy, doing layouts, and working with art and graphic materials are explained in Part II of this book.

Most stores, of course, will not be able to support an internal advertising department. In that case, the functions outlined on the organization chart (Figure 7) will be shared by the headquarter advertising department and the local store manager's office.

3

Corporate Planning

Advertising should not be planned in a vacuum. A store's or chain's advertising plans are linked very closely, of course, to sales and budget expectations. Therefore, let us review some of the chain-wide planning that must go along with advertising.

THE ADVANCE PLANNING SCHEDULE

Both a multi-unit chain and the single store operation must begin advance planning with a schedule. The planning schedule is created by two people, the merchandise manager and the advertising manager or their respective offices.

The retailer actually should have two planning schedules. The first, for "Spring," covers the promotional months February through July. The second schedule covers the months August through January, retailing's "Fall" season. *The deadline date for completion of each of these schedules is most important and should be established early and communicated to all concerned.* Each

6 Month Planning Schedule Fall, August through January

Promotional Month	Aug.	Sept.	Oct.	Nov./Dec.	Jan.
Aug. Sept. Oct. Nov./Dec. Jan.					
Planning Meeting					
Planning Guidance and Instruction Letter Released to all Department Managers					
First Review Meeting					
Second Review Meeting					
Departmental Review Meetings					
Finalized 6 Month Calendar Released to Stores					
Departmental Message Pages For Planning Guide and Merchandise Offering Pages Due to Advertising Dept.					
Planning Guide to Printer					
Planning Guide & Promotional Package Ship to Stores					
Promotional Package in Stores					
Store Release Order Date					
Source Earliest Ship Date					

Figure 8

schedule should be completed approximately six to nine months in advance of the season's first promotional month. The specific advance time depends, of course, on the size of the company, merchandise availability, and shipping factors.

Figure 8 shows a sample of a typical advance planning schedule. To establish deadline dates for each of the steps listed, work backwards from the last deadline specified. For example, in many stores the last deadline would be the merchandise "ship date." If it takes six weeks for goods to reach the store (this will vary depending on the chain's supply sources), then six weeks must be counted back from the desired "in-store" date. Counting back from that date will give the "ship date" deadline.

If the retailer wants four weeks to review the corporate monthly promotion package and finalize store promotion and advertising plans before releasing item orders, he should establish the planning guide in-store date and count back four weeks to arrive at "shipment of planning package to store" date. If he must have the planning package in the store by that specific date, then he must count back the number of weeks it takes to mail and print it. This will give the "to printer" deadline.

Applying these time requirements to each step in the procedure, the initial planning meeting date for each promotional month can be determined. During the early stages of planning, some companies plan two or three months at one time. However, it is usually best to plan one month at a time. There is one important exception; November and December should always be planned and programmed as one promotional package.

The advance time required for completing a meaningful advertising/promotional program may startle many. But when you realize the ordering and receiving factors involved, it will become obvious why so much time is needed.

The steps listed on the planning schedule illustrated in Figure 8 do not in any way represent a listing that would be correct for every retailer. The retailer must make a planning schedule meaningful to his specific company's size and methods. However, to make the schedule work, regardless of how complex it is, the deadline dates must be mandatory for all people concerned—all executives, all supervisors, etc. This can be accomplished only if the schedule and its deadlines are supported fully by the top management of the company.

SALES BUDGETS

All operating, sales promotion, and advertising budgets for a store are based on departmental sales budgets. For this very simple and basic reason, sales budgets must be both accurate and realistic.

The department manager prepares his estimated sales budget for a six-month period. Most stores have initial sales budgets prepared for a year or possibly two or three years, but these must be adjusted to current trends. The six-month period is the time to finalize to realistic figures. Then, about six weeks before each month begins, further adjustments may be made. If the six-month projections are on target, these monthly adjustments are usually minor. The budget completion dates vary with different companies, according to company size and methods. However, in order for nonselling departments to prepare their budgets, the time element required may be five or seven months in advance of the first promotional month of the period.

To help a department arrive at the most accurate budget possible, most companies issue bulletins, memos, letters, and/or a coordinated departmental schedule which give marketing guidelines for the sales period. Departmental guidance and information are given for seasonal expansion or contraction, current sales trends, important lines of goods for the season, industry trends, departmental percent recommended for promotional goods, economic trends, and company averages for previous years. Markup expectations for specific lines of goods and recommended advertising ratios to sales also are given. One very important item is the recommended percent of increase or decrease of sales for each department.

For the smaller company, marketing information from the Chamber of Commerce or federal government will have to be utilized. The major newspapers in every market also have figures available that will help departments prepare meaningful sales budgets.

ESTIMATING SALES

Estimating sales is a serious and difficult task. Doing a sales budget is not simply applying a slight optimistic increase to last year's actual figures. The department manager must know from where he can expect sales and in what lines specifically. He must be able to pinpoint where any decreases might be and how they can be made up.

If desired sales are out of reach or, at best, cannot equal last year's sales, then the adjustment must be made at the time the initial budgets are being developed. Budgeting "even" in inflationary times or budgeting a percent of increase comparable to the inflation rate is, in truth, budgeting fewer transactions.

PLANNING IN THE GIANT CHAINS COMPARED TO SMALLER CHAINS

The efficient decentralized large chain store does have a competitive advantage over smaller, local competition because it receives a completely planned monthly advertising package from the central office that costs considerably more than the store is charged back for it. Secondly, the co-op advertising effort exceeds that of the smaller retailer. Other than these two advantages, however, the large chain store has no other, at least none that the smaller store or independent could not duplicate to its own scale.

One disadvantage of the large chain is that it must be almost totally committed to advance plans and often does not have the flexibility to adjust or to move quickly on a special promotion or current sales trend. A second disadvantage is that the larger retailer is required to carry broader assortments to retain a competitive position. When the large chain tries to reduce its assortments, it risks its competitive edge. A small retailer has more flexibility with inventory dollars. The opportunities for departmental expansion and contraction are much greater than the large chain's even though it seems at times that the giant chains have developed more expertise in this merchandise function.

THE PROMOTION FUND

A retailer can gain a competitive edge by designating, for purposes of a "Promotion Fund," a small fixed percentage on the cost of all goods ordered by each department. The percent designated would be one percent or one-half of one percent of the cost of the item, each item varying within this range.

Manufacturers' co-op (co-operative advertising) funds can be placed in the departmental promotion fund. Co-op money is given by a manufacturer to a store to subsidize ads that feature that manufacturer's products. The manufacturer charges a fixed percentage on the cost of all of his items sold to the store. This money is returned in the form of cash payments to subsidize the cost of the ad or in the form of credits. To use co-op monies as part of the promotion fund, the store must request that the manufacturer give the earned co-op dollars in the form of credits to be applied to the specific items and department. (The retailer using a promotion fund has already charged the department a fixed percentage for all items ordered.) By this means, the retailer has complete flexibility with any co-op advertising money.

Uses of the Promotion Fund

The promotion fund has many uses. It affords the retailer the opportunity to move best-selling goods at reduced sale prices and to subsidize the cost of advertising these items—in newspaper ads or special direct mail circulars, or whatever promotion media necessary.

Total 100 percent paid newspaper ads can be developed from the promotion fund by using those co-op monies designated for specific merchandise. Even such large promotional events such as grand openings can be subsidized from the fund.

If a determined, storewide special campaign is planned, it too can be paid for partly through the promotion fund. In this way the total financial burden of a special campaign is not placed on the store's or specific departments' promotion and/or advertising budgets. Such a campaign can include item cost reductions, a variety of departmental co-op advertising plans, and special merchandise buys at featured prices.

The promotion fund would be very useful in counter-attacking a competitor's campaign or leadership position in one or more merchandise areas. In addition, the fund can be used to assist financing departmental sales contests.

The promotion fund can indeed be a very important tool in the development of each department's contribution to company profitability.

It Can Be Done

Many may argue against a promotion fund, saying that a relatively high percentage of net sales are allocated for advertising on a regular basis. They may say that there is no way to allocate another half or quarter of one percent of cost of goods for a promotional fund. However, one thing to avoid doing is "percenting" yourself out of the profit column. The retailer is in business to make a profit. But he is also in business to maintain his profit percentage. If a company fails to achieve increasing volume each year, it will be in trouble eventually.

Advertising alone is not enough to keep this growth rate going year after year. The retailer must develop the means that will assure his store(s) a competitive merchandising edge. The promotion fund will help achieve this. If there is no other way to afford it, the retailer can adjust his advertising ratio downwards slightly. This will build the promotional fund which makes large dollar amounts available when they are most needed.

CHECKLIST OF BASIC PLANNING REQUIREMENTS

The retailer must have certain information in order to finalize his advance advertising plans. These requirements are:

- Last year's sales vs. previous year's, by department
- Last year's special event sales by department; departmental percentages compared to total store
- List of this year's calendar changes and holidays compared to last year's
- This year's promotion calendar compared to last year's
- List of major competitor events
- List of major competitor key items or line promotions of last year
- List of important municipal events that have retail tie-ins
- List of scheduled newspaper special sections
- Tearsheets of past ads compared to those of key competitors

- Budgeted departmental sales this year
- Budgeted event sales this year
- Marketing facts guidance and information
- Last year's storewide event contests and departmental contests

The retailer's success in advance planning can be measured largely by how well he does his homework in compiling the above items and putting the information he gathers to the best use.

THE SIX-MONTH PLANNING BOOK

Without a six-month plan, the corporate advertising department could not plan or prepare ads in sufficient advance time. And without the plan, the advertising manager and staff on the store level could not adequately budget or plan for store sales and promotions. Some chains plan on a 12-month basis, but, because of quickly changing market patterns in today's economy, the "season" approach is becoming more and more realistic for most retailers.

A coordinated package or book of the finalized six-month plan is released to stores and headquarter departments from the central advertising department. It covers all the pertinent facts about the program:

- A copy of the six-month advance planning schedule
- Memo or letter from the corporate advertising manager listing highlights and general strategy for the season
- Calendar changes from last year
- Departmental event list with running dates
- Circulars and/or pre-prints available and costs
- Co-op advertising programs available
- Calendar page for each of the six months with each special event noted and comments on optional events and supplemental advertising available

For the chain store with a decentralized advertising structure, local scheduling of pre-printed newspaper sections is optional. It is also up to the individual store how much emphasis is placed on specific promotions the corporate advertising office includes in its six-month program.

PRE-PRINT SECTIONS

Orders for corporate pre-printed newspaper sections or circulars must be obtained from participating stores early. Tied in with a corporate subsidy program, a pre-printed section or circular costing three dollars or $3.50 per thousand copies will be quite attractive to many of the chain's stores.

Stores sometimes feel, however, that a circular or pre-print is nothing more than a buying office means to spread more goods to more stores. When a store commits itself to a pre-print, it must stock every item that has been placed in it, and this can contribute to inventory buildup in excess of budgets for some stores. Constant domination of pre-prints in an advertising program is not considered wise.

The three dollars per thousand or whatever attractive price is offered should not be the determining factor for a store to schedule a pre-print. A review should be made of all items to see whether they are appropriate to the store's specific market. Since store profits are figured on turns, there is always a reluctance to order items known to be slow movers in a particular store. This reluctance is understandable, as is the persistance of the central corporate office in "selling" the pre-prints to stores (often the corporate advertising manager will personally visit key stores to get their commitment). However, if packed too full with non-movers, pre-prints eventually can affect the inventory position of the total company.

THE SIX-MONTH CALENDAR

Each month of the six-month period will be finalized in monthly planning meetings scheduled on the advance planning schedule. But first the final calendar of events for the entire six months is completed five to seven months in advance of the six month promotional period. This advance completion time for the

Promotion Calendar

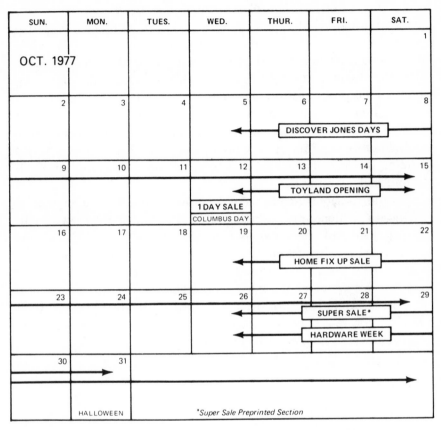

SUN.	MON.	TUES.	WED.	THUR.	FRI.	SAT.
OCT. 1977						1
2	3	4	5	6	7	8
				◄ DISCOVER JONES DAYS		
9	10	11	12	13	14	15
			TOYLAND OPENING →			
			1 DAY SALE			
			COLUMBUS DAY			
16	17	18	19	20	21	22
			◄ HOME FIX UP SALE			
23	24	25	26	27	28	29
			◄ SUPER SALE* →			
			◄ HARDWARE WEEK			
30	31					
	HALLOWEEN		*Super Sale Preprinted Section			

RELATED ITEM PROMOTIONS:
HOME FIX-UP SALE   10/12-10/29
(Depts: 00, 00, 00, 00, 00)

DEPARTMENT PROMOTIONS
TOYLAND OPENING   10/12-10/15
(Dept: 00)
HARDWARE WEEK . 10/26-11/5
(Dept: 00)

MAJOR STOREWIDE PROMOTIONS
DISCOVER JONES DAYS 10/5-10/15
ONE DAY SALE (OPTIONAL) 10/12
SUPER SALE 10/26-10/31

Figure 9

calendar is necessary so that it can be considered in the monthly merchandise meetings, at which time items for each event are finalized.

The reviewing time of scheduled events will be about two months, with the last of the monthly reviews completed approximately three months before the seasonal period begins. Then, while the actual advertising materials are being prepared in the corporate office, the stores in the field finalize their own six-month plans, deciding which programs to participate in and which ones to pass by.

When you consider that a store will receive its six-month "Fall" calendar sometime in April or May, approximately seven months before the important Christmas selling season, the advance planning and preparation time afforded all stores becomes an obvious and real advantage.

The six-month event calendar (see Figure 9 for a sample of one month's calendar) is developed and finalized through tough-minded review of the previous year, last year's calendar, and last year's "real" results. Disappointments are looked at, but a deeper look must be given to causes. Before a previous year's events are changed, last year's errors must be searched out. If new sales and advertising events are to replace old, they must be supported with reliable information as to why the new promotional events will be improvements in total advertising planning.

4

Departmental Advertising Budgets

Good advertising plans always begin with accurate budgets. If a retailer is part of a corporate chain that publishes a marketing guide for purposes of sales budgeting, he will have a higher probability of on target departmental sales estimates. If unrealistic sales budgets must be adjusted later, so must the advertising schedule, and this could prove disastrous.

Not only must sales budgets be accurate, but they must also be closely adhered to when the advertising budget is being developed. However, there are times for an educated "gamble" for sales in excess of the actual budget. If an advertising program is developed for a "sleeper" or under-par department, there must be flexibility that allows for trimming if the actual sales fall short of expectations. "Locked in" expenditures which cannot be adjusted to a poor sales result will require a cut in the following month's schedule in order to adjust the year-to-date advertising ratio. The end result will be a weakening of the retailer's total program.

Sales budgeting is not really advertising in the pure sense, but the sales budget directly affects advertising and, in many cases, is the culprit behind unreasonable amounts of newspaper lineage reductions and item changes at a later date.

ADVERTISING RATIOS TO SALES

Departmental advertising ratios to sales and the departmental advertising budget are determined by the store advertising manager, or, if there is none, by the store manager. Whichever manager determines a department's six-month advertising ratio to sales, he should carefully review his figures with the department managers before finalizing them.

The department's advertising budget is arrived at by applying the advertising ratio as a percentage to the department's six-month budgeted figure. This represents the department's six-month dollar advertising budget. The total advertising dollars for all departments add up to the store's advertising budget. Dividing the stores total budgeted sales figure into the total departmental budgeted advertising dollars should yield the store's monthly advertising ratio.

The store budget will cover all advertising costs including the "home office charge" for monthly advertising service materials, advertising department fixed and variable expenses, and advertising department payroll. The departmental costs for all items other than the actual cost of newspaper space and air time is usually only about one-half of one percent of the advertising ratio. It is lineage and air time that take the major chunk out of the advertising budget. For example, if a department's advertising ratio is 2.5 percent of sales, the department will use about two percent for newspaper space and air time.

Advertising ratios for each department will differ. There is no correct ratio for a department that is consistent for all stores, but there are sufficient guidelines to go by. The determination of the departmental advertising ratio depends on local market conditions, competition, the size and types of the retailer's departments, his specific objectives for departments, and other factors.

Departmental advertising ratios generally supported by the industry and various trade associations are as follows:

Furniture	2.0	Garden Shop	2.3
Domestics	3.0	Tires	2.0
Gift Shop	1.8	Shoes	1.8
Housewares	2.3	Infants wear	2.0
Sewing Machines and		Women's Dresses, Robes	1.8
Vacuum Cleaners	2.0	Men's Furnishings	1.9
Laundry Appliances	1.7	Hosiery	2.1
Refrigeration	2.3	Girls Wear	2.7
Electric/Gas Stoves	1.9	Millinery	3.2
Sporting Goods	1.9	Stationery, Books	3.0
Automotive Accessories	2.0	Jewelry	2.7
Toys	2.3	Drugs	2.7
Candy	2.0	Notions	1.7
Men's Work Clothing	1.5	Women's Accessories	3.0
Hardware	1.7	Lingerie	2.7
Pet Shop	2.7	Yard Goods	2.0
Electrical	2.0	Corsets, Foundations	2.3
Plumbing and Heating	1.7	Women's Coats, Suits	3.0
Wallpaper	3.0	Women's Blouses,	
Building Materials	1.7	Sportswear	1.7

The figures shown are found fairly consistently among major chains. Retailers might want to check other industry figures to find the correct or happy medium for their own departments. Independent stores' ratios for advertising would be higher because their ad preparation costs are not shared by several stores through one central location.

Advertising ratios also vary by department because each department's characteristics are not the same as its neighbors. In addition, each department in a general merchandise store has specific goals. For example, the appliance department produces many volume dollars but very few people. With its high volume dollars, this department can be productive with a smaller advertising ratio than, for instance, the domestics department. The domestics department volume is considerably lower, but it attracts more people into the store. Because traffic is important to the store, this department will demand a higher advertising ratio.

SIX MONTH DEPARTMENTAL WORKSHEET

DEPT.		% to __		% to __		% to __		% to __		% to __		% to __	TOTAL SEASON
Total Soft Lines													
Total Home Furnish.													
Total Hard Lines													
Total Appliances													
Total Specialty													
Grand Total													

% to Key: 1-Season, 2-Total Month.

Figure 10

CHARTING ADVERTISING EXPENDITURES
TO BUDGETED SALES PATTERNS

Having determined the advertising ratio for each of his departments and arriving at an advertising budget for each, the retailer's next step is to chart budgeted sales by department for the six-month period. In this way, the *monthly* departmental advertising budget will be determined.

Using a worksheet similar to the one shown in Figure 10, the advertising manager lists budgeted sales for each month. The total six-month budgeted sales figure for a department represents 100 percent. This total is divided into each month's budgeted sales to determine a percentage which is indicated on the chart with a dot. Lines are drawn connecting each dot to give a pattern of sales.

Sales patterns are different for every department. For this reason, the short cut of charting total store sales and planning advertising to the store's total advertising *dollars* will result in lost departmental sales opportunities and missed budgets. Advertising should be planned on the basis of a *ratio* of advertising dollars spent to department budgeted sales.

The next step is to chart the basic advertising expenditure for each of the six months for every department. The prime objective is to have enough advertising money available for all departments at the times they need it—at the beginning of a peak sales pattern and during it. If corporate events do not tie into this period of time, then the appropriate adjustment should be made on the corporate calendar.

Figure 11 is an example of a chart of advertising expenditures to a department's budgeted sales pattern. Advertising dollars are charted or allocated to the consumer's buying pattern (budgeted sales) so that advertising pressure can be applied at the start of the selling peak and during it.

Applying the same advertising ratio to sales for every month is not advisable. The name of the retailing game is "turns"—how many times you can turn your average inventory. To do this successfully, among other means, you must "shoot the ducks when they are flying" by ensuring a sufficient amount of ad dollars for peak promotional periods for each department.

Reviewing the initial charting results, it might be apparent

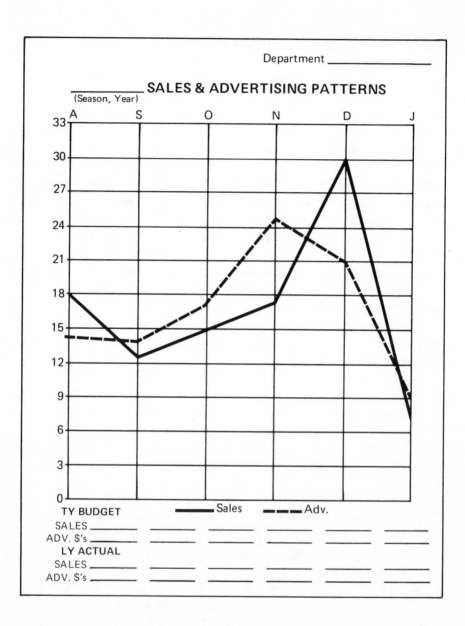

Figure 11

that some departmental monthly ratios are not realistic. For example, for one month there may be a five or ten percent advertising ratio which, of course, is considerably above the generally-accepted norm. Departmental advertising ratios can legitimately be high for some months which is why the retailer charts advertising dollars —to be able to spend money when it will be the most productive. However, a total store six month advertising budget should never exceed three to four percent except for a big event such as a grand opening.

The store's advertising total also must be reviewed and compared to the six-month budgeted advertising ratio. If it does not compare favorably, adjustments must be made. Adjustments made at this point will head off major problems later. The budgeted advertising ratio is a commitment for the six-month period. If it is 2.5 percent, this means that at the end of the period, the year-to-date store advertising ratio must balance out at 2.5 percent. Some months will have a 3.5 percent ratio, others a 1.7 or 2.1, but at the close of the six months, the ratio must come out to 2.5.

ADVERTISING BUDGET CONTROL

When the final advertising schedule is written, the advertising manager will have a comprehensive accounting to the last dollar of what is allocated to each department. He will also have the budgeted sales for each department. Control of the advertising budget is accomplished by keeping strict watch on ratio expenditure to sales, by department.

During the month, the advertising manager or store manager carefully checks the weekly and daily departmental sales report for sales that fail to meet or those that beat last year's figures. If there is a seriously depressed sales trend developing in any one of the departments, he will consult immediately with the department manager to determine cause. If sales performance cannot be corrected immediately, that department's advertising lineage will be cut to the level of its current sales. If sales are being missed by ten percent, for example, advertising lineage will be cut accordingly. When the problem is corrected, more dollars for lineage will be given to the department; however, these dollars will be based on a newly revised budget sales figure.

At the initial stage of budgeting, it is important to realize the seriousness and difficulty in controlling an advertising expenditure to a predetermined budget figure. The professional advertising managers of the biggest chains and stores have their own "insurance" policy for this problem—at the very early stages of budget planning they will deduct for each month an amount equivalent to ten to 15 percent of the total budgeted advertising dollars and hold this money in reserve.

The advertising manager can use these funds throughout the month as they are needed. To accelerate lagging sales, for instance, he might go after large volume the quickest possible way, through his furniture or big ticket appliance departments; he will have the funds to increase advertising space or frequency for just such contingencies. There are other unknowns that present themselves each month, a special buy which needs advertising support, a decision to add color to a newspaper layout, etc. The advertising budget cushion covers these unknowns.

A common error to avoid is carrying over excessive advertising expenditures into the next month. This does nothing at all except weaken future promotional efforts. If any expenditure is over the monthly budget, and many times it is, the price must be paid in that particular month.

5

The Store Advertising Budget

DEVELOPING THE BUDGET

The six-month advertising budget for the store is the sum total of all budgeted expenditures for all store departments. The first step in developing this budget is to finalize the six-month promotional calendar. Using a blank calendar form similar to the one shown in Figure 12, the advertising manager pencils in the following information:

- This year's dates and holidays
- Past two years' daily total store sales
- Any additional (other than corporate) local storewide events with start and end dates
- All departmental events and related-department events
- All supplemental events (preview nights, one-day sales, etc.)

YOUR DAILY PROMOTIONAL PLANS

SUNDAY	MONDAY	TUESDAY	WEDNESDAY	THURSDAY	FRIDAY	SATURDAY

Figure 12

- Total sales for each week compared to past two years' and the appropriate percentages (larger stores would give a finer breakdown by departmental group showing percentage of each group to week's total store sale)

With all other required reference materials within easy reach—last years' advertising schedule, departmental sales and advertising budgets, sales and advertising pattern charts, notes on competition, and corporate promotional information, the advertising manager is ready to spot on each month's calendar the anticipated major expenditures.

The first step is converting budgeted departmental newspaper advertising expenses into column inch figures. For most retailers, the newspaper is still the major advertising medium and represents an expenditure equal to 50 to 70 percent of the store's total advertising budget. Since it is the major medium, newspaper lineage is planned first. The advertising manager's objective is to arrive at the approximate number of pages or half-page units each department and group of related departments will use in newspaper advertising each month.

The important point to remember is, at this stage, the advertising manager is not writing the monthly advertising schedule; rather he is finalizing his six-month budget. Before he can finalize it, however, he must be certain he has allocated sufficient money for support of each of the promotional months. In addition, he must make an early decision regarding commitments to pre-printed newspaper advertising sections.

The costs of pre-prints are taken from major media dollars. If taking a pre-print weakens a newspaper advertising campaign, it probably should not be ordered. If the advertising manager feels the pre-print will add impact to his total advertising effort, he will order it.

When the major media allocations of advertising dollars are completed, other expenditures are added: radio and television, direct mail, and other advertising media. Then, other fixed and variable operating costs are added, and the total is the monthly advertising budget.

Every dollar to be spent and charged to advertising must be budgeted. At this stage the advertising manager will have a basic six-month advertising program and budget for the store. The department advertising schedule has not yet been finalized; only the "group" space has been allocated. The department advertising schedules are written before each promotional month.

A MAJOR BUDGETING DIFFERENCE AMONG CHAINS

The next point in budget consideration is a very important one for every retailer. The question to consider is: Which should take precedence, the budgeted advertising dollars or the budgeted advertising percent? Major chains do it both ways. Some believe that the best way is to make the percent mandatory because this makes for easier control, allowing for additional ads to be scheduled when sales are accelerating.

Other retailers believe the realization of increased sales and coming in under a budgeted dollar expenditure adds to the store's net profit column. This is true, and if there is no real need to schedule additional unbudgeted ads, it should not be done. However, if there is an opportunity to keep accelerated sales moving, and more goods are received and sold quickly, the store will add more dollars to the profit column if additional ads are scheduled. This can best be done with the percent method.

CORPORATE BUDGET GUIDANCE

Guidance for the store's seasonal advertising budget should be received from the headquarter office three or four months before the six-month period begins. Corporate guidance, again, will vary with company. It generally consists of supplying the budget forms, instructions for distribution, deadline dates, announcement of the corporate advertising service charges to be budgeted, and a detailed summary of promotional highlights for each of the six months. Important economic trends are given as they relate to each department and line of goods. Expected sales increases or decreases also are given as well as recommended ad ratios for the departments.

CAREFUL ADVANCE PLANNING

The six-month budget can be completed in any amount of time, from one day to four weeks. What is put into it is exactly what the store will get out of it. If a department's advertising dollars are not protected, you can be assured that the department's advertising program will fall far short of its mark.

Putting all eggs into one basket is to be avoided. If a department's advertising budget for August is $980, it would be highly questionable to allocate $840 of that amount for participation in a pre-print. The department manager would be placing all advertising dollars into one major effort. To come up with a three percent advertising ratio, he would have to realize $28,000 in sales from the specials the pre-print announces.

This type of error in decision can be avoided by reviewing the department's sales objectives for six months instead of one and then looking at each specific month as one campaign to achieve that month's budgeted sales. There is a time for pre-print participation and there are times for other special expenditures, but they must be planned for carefully.

THE MONTHLY ADVERTISING BUDGET

The six-month budget (see Figure 13 for an example of a budget format) is a base, a protective base for the budgeting of advertising money. Each month of the six-month period is subject to change; however, due to the initial work already put into the six-month plans by corporate headquarters and the store itself, changes will be minor. Eighty percent of the planning work will have been done already. When the final advertising schedule is written 30 to 60 days before each promotional month, the task is simply one of finalizing, not one of first drafts.

Monthly Budget Control

The budget for the month must be complete in every detail, listing all costs to the penny. The monthly budget form corresponds to the six-month form. Each of the classifications on the form must

SIX MONTH ADVERTISING BUDGET   Period_____19_____

LINE	EXPENDITURE CLASSIFICATION	PROMOTIONAL MONTH						TOTAL PERIOD
1.	Newspaper Space							
2.	Newspaper Inserts							
3.	Less Credits							
4.	Total Newspaper (1+2-3)							
5.	Radio/Television							
6.	Billboards							
7.	Circulars							
8.	Direct Mail							
9.	Total Supplemental Media (5+6+7+8)							
10.	Total All Media (4+9)							
11.	Consumer Literature							
12.	Yellow Pages							
13.	Regional, Nat'l Advertising							
14.	Credit Inserts							
15.	Catalogs							
16.	Total Other Advertising (11 thru 15)							
17.	Payroll							
18.	Artwork Purchases							
19.	Association Costs							
20.	National Office Charge							
21.	Miscellaneous							
22.	Total Fixed Expenses (17 thru 21)							
23.	TOTAL ADVERTISING COST (10+16+22)							
24.	Budgeted Net Sales							
25.	Budgeted Advertising % to Sales							

Figure 13

ADVERTISING PURCHASE ORDER   124578

1

THE GREAT RETAILER
CENTER STREET
TOWN, CITY, USA 00134

Publication Date _____

TO:

Acct. No. _____
Job No. _____
Job Title _____

_____

Quantity	DESCRIPTION	Price	Cost
	Terms _____		

Purchase order number must appear on all invoices. Corrections, changes or additions are restricted to the individual responsible for the specific job commitment. Make no changes in price, terms, delivery date, quantity, or quality specifications without his written consent. Bid prices are accepted as a firm price. No charge for packing, boxing, shipping or mailing will be allowed unless previously specified.

Date _____   _____
Advertising Manager

Figure 14

be supported by a detailed accounting sheet explaining the specific cost breakdown of the item and/or items for that classification.

There are three major requirements for good control:

1. If there are additions to the budget, comparable dollars must be cut from somewhere else in the budget.

2. There must be a separate and exclusive advertising purchase order, similar to the one illustrated in Figure 14. This purchase order should be numbered and attached to every ad released. It should be issued for any and all purchases to be charged to the advertising account. A three-copy system is suggested. The first copy is given to the source of the purchase; the second and third copies are placed in an open order file. When the invoice is received, the second copy is attached to the invoice and released for payment. The third copy is attached to the duplicate invoice marked "Release for Payment on ——" and filed by month.

3. A ledger sheet should be completed listing each of the days of the month, with columns designated for the expenditure budgeted for each day, the month-to-date budgeted figure, plus a blank column for listing daily actual and daily month-to-date actual expenditures. Month-to-date sales should be listed, and the advertising cost percent of sales given. The responsibility for this ledger should be given to one person, usually the bookkeeper.

With these three controls, adherence to the pre-determined advertising budget will be considerably easier. While sales trends are extremely important, the advertising manager must not over-react to them or he might experience lost sales. If a sales trend shows a ten percent decrease, for example, the astute advertising manager does not cut expenditures until he finds out where the decrease is coming from. If he delays or does not notice the trend early enough, he will, unfortunately, also have to cut his expenditures in other areas that are doing well.

Being alert to budget expectations and keeping up with daily sales figures are important aspects of the advertising manager's job.

THE SAFETY CUSHION

Approximately ten percent should be deducted from all department budgets for a safety cushion, mentioned in the previous chapter. This contingency fund can be used to pull a budget back into balance when and if it is necessary.

Some departments do not require advertising except in peak seasons and some require none at all. One such department is the catalog desk; another, the repair department. These sales must be included in the total store sales figures, however, which gives the advertising manager another cushion. Although some operators may disagree, including these departments in total store sales figures for purposes of budgeting is correct because such departments do benefit from store advertising, although indirectly.

The big ticket volume departments provide a base without which the advertising department would be hard pressed. Big ticket departments are an advertising manager's best friends. Many times, when the ad budget has gone over, the manager can depend on these departments to pull the necessary added sales volume before the budget period ends. Sometimes special promotions will be run in these departments to pull up total store sales.

Another source for cushion is co-op advertising (see Chapter 3). When a department has co-op advertising funds available, these should be used and should not in any way replace the regular advertising efforts.

The point to remember is that the budget must be met, either the budgeted dollar expenditure or the budgeted percent. Departmental budgets seldom hit their budgeted monthly percentages; they are always just a little over or a little under. The important requirement is that they meet their budgeted six-month figure.

6

The Advertising Schedule

Up to now, we have discussed budgets, planning schedules, organization, and structures, but have talked little about the consumer. How can he or she be reached? How does he react to advertising? How can he be persuaded to visit the store more often? How can more consumers within a store's market be enticed into the store?

All of these questions must be answered by the store or advertising manager when he develops the advertising schedule. This schedule lists the dates ads are to run, thus planning the proper timing of merchandise presentation to the consumer. It can be the most overlooked, underrated, and misunderstood component of effective retail advertising.

WRITING THE SCHEDULE

The secret of writing a workable advertising schedule is putting all the pieces together to work towards one end. The first

```
WORLD'S GREATEST RETAILER

FIRST WEEK MAY 1975 ADVERTISING SCHEDULE

              Friday, May 2 (Mother's Day Specials, Fri., Sat. Only)
                  Women's Apparel-100" ................ 5 col x 20 Times
Color ad          Electrical Housewares-60" .............. 4 col x 15 Star

              Sunday, May 4
                  Furniture-172" .................. 8 col x Full Star
                  Appliances-88" .................. 4 col x Full Star
Rotogravure   Women's Apparel-70" ............. 5 col x 14" Star Mag.

              Wednesday, May 7 (Super Sale Days—Ends Saturday)
                  Apparel: 10-20", 14-36", 24-18", 18-24"  ...... )
                  Women's Acces.: 24-12", 11-18", 3-24"  ....... ) 172" Star

              Thursday, May 8 (Super Sale—Ends Saturday)
                  P.U. 5/7 Apparel, Women's Acces. Page  ....... 172" Times
                  Automotive 61-36", 64-60", 28-18" .......... 120" Star
```

TYPING THE AD SCHEDULE

All stores have different format approaches to typing the finalized ad schedule for a promotional month. The schedule is actually two examples. Through Sunday lists the breakdown of space by department name and specific ad column size. The lower half of the schedule lists the breakdown of space by group identification, then by department number. Total inches are indicated but not the specific column ad size. This leaves the layout department some flexibility, particularly for the chain store. For the chain store there may be a perfect ad in the current or past ad service book that meets the merchandise strategy desired, but it may be 40 inches additional in size or 20 inches less than what is scheduled. The store will pick up the ready-made ad rather than lock itself into a predetermined ad size calling for new prep.

The ad schedule should be very specific with only required information. Special ads that require special handling and/or earlier deadlines, rotogravure and/or color ads are flagged out conspicuously as a danger or alert signal. The schedule is written and typed for the complete promotional month. The department manager will review the schedule, circling the specific inches designated for his department. The schedule serves as notification to the department manager this is the space he must merchandise.

Figure 15

requirement is to have the schedule written by and the responsibility of one individual, either the store manager or the advertising manager if there is one. He is responsible for scheduling ads according to the needs of his store.

Several vital factors must be considered in developing the schedule. The first is determination of important departments for each month for the purpose of planning a total store mix and knowing exactly where the bulk of total store sales will come from. A promotion program exclusively geared to dollar volume is not enough; nor is the continuous promotion of low end sale departments to generate traffic. The total store promotional strategy, to be effective, must have departmental balance. The advertising or store manager must make certain that such a balanced mix is represented in the advertising schedule. Figure 15 shows a sample schedule.

DETERMINING THE MONTH'S BIG DEPARTMENTS

Using a worksheet, the store or advertising manager reviews the budgeted sales column for the month and designates the ten top volume departments in the store. Next, he designates the top ten departments in transactions. The top ten net profit departments are identified next. Then, the departments that are expected to experience a sales peak during the month are singled out. If it is a smaller store, the same procedure would be applied to merchandise lines.

On a new worksheet, all top ten departments in each category are listed. Across the page, they are divided into four appropriate categories: volume, transactions, profit, and peaks. An "X" is placed in each of the columns for the appropriate departments. If a retail store has 40 or more departments, the list may total up to 25 different departments which qualify in one of the four categories. Of this amount, possibly 50 percent or more would be in the top ten in more than one category. These are the departments which will keynote the retailer's success for that specific month.

These departments will give the store its required mix and balance; they therefore warrant the store manager's undivided attention. He will schedule these departments first. At all costs, the top departments' budgets must be protected. If additional advertising money is available that month, they will be given to the departments with the best expectations because if these departments meet their budgeted sales expectations, so will the total store.

SCHEDULING THE FIVE AD TYPES

The next important factor in scheduling is the assurance that each of the top departments has a proper advertising mix. Of all ads published, most can be identified as one of five types:

- The omnibus ad (storewide ad, featuring items from all departments)
- The line promotion ad (featuring the "good," "better," and "best" pieces of merchandise in a particular line)
- The related item ad (featuring related items from different departments)
- The tonnage ad (featuring one item, stocked in large quantities, at a very special price)
- The departmental ad (showing items from one department—featuring a wide variety of merchandise)

Why these different types of ads?

- The omnibus ad produces storewide traffic
- The line promotion ad gives the opportunity to present low-end, middle, and top-of-the line merchandise in an attempt to appeal to all segments of the market
- The related item ad promotes intra-department traffic
- The tonnage ad produces volume and traffic
- The department ad establishes the department as "headquarters" for particular items, produces volume, profits, and traffic

Just as the store would be in error to promote only one department each month and expect storewide success, a department cannot restrict its promotional effort to one ad type. If success with one kind of ad were possible at all times, the omnibus ad would be scheduled for every advertising day of the month. The omnibus ad, for a period of time, will pay its way, but a department requires more than only traffic or high volume. Ideally, it should have both. A well-planned monthly schedule for a department would include participation in an omnibus ad, a tie-in with another department for a related item ad, a free-standing line promotion ad, and a department ad with representative items that shows a wide variety of merchandise assortments. If the budget permits, a tonnage ad could be added to this list.

In writing the advertising schedule, the advertising manager should schedule departmental space around the major events—the important selling days of the month for each department. Daily sales expectations for each department will be his guide in making this schedule.

YARDSTICKS

Advertising schedules cannot in themselves change consumer buying patterns. The schedule may improve a departmental sales pattern, but it will do so according to the consumer's own pattern of buying. To schedule ads to take the best advantage of consumer patterns, the retailer must use all the yardsticks available to him. The first and most important of these is last year's total store daily sales. If nothing is planned or scheduled to meet or beat a particularly heavy last year sales figure, the store can count on a sales decrease.

If there is an especially heavy day to beat, the advertising manager must review last year's departmental sales report for that specific day to establish from which departments the sales came. Was the increase across the board involving all departments or was it just a few? In either case, he must check last year's advertising schedule and tearsheets. A like program or a stronger one must be developed and scheduled for this year.

Here are some ways to come up with a worthwhile advertising schedule:

1. Review the current year-to-date sales figures by department. Have those departments with sales decreases, compared to last year's efforts, received additional and /or special attention in this year's schedule?

2. Review the year's/month's top ten departments' newspaper lineage compared to last year's/month's actual lineage expenditures. Are they the same or better?

3. Compare lineage or media commitments for this year's holiday weekends with last year's. Are the required additional lineage, pre-prints, or air time scheduled?

4. Review, in depth, the total sales promotion program for those departments in their peak selling seasons. If these are correct, good storewide traffic will be assured.

5. Compare last year's advertising report to this year's schedule. Are all departments receiving as many ad dollars and as much newspaper lineage/radio-TV time as they did last year? Are all receiving their rightful share? (It is usually the case that in comparing figures to the previous year, most departmental sales decrease percentages can be matched almost equally to the percentage of reduced newspaper lineage.)

6. Review last year's supplemental media efforts and compare to this year's planned effort. Are this year's efforts weak and separate or are they a part of the total strategy, supporting and strengthening the major media effort. One without the other will make each that much weaker. Together, both will be that much stronger.

7. Review this year's scheduled total column inches for each department. Do they correspond to the specific budget figure?

The advertising schedule represents an investment of net profit dollars for the retailer; for this reason, time spent in review is never wasted. The advertising manager must write a schedule that produces the most sales possible.

PRE-SEASON ADVERTISING

Pre-season advertising, usually restricted to big ticket seasonal items, pre-sells to the consumer for a very short, but peak, high volume selling period. Little immediate dollar volume is obtained from pre-season advertising, but the advance publicity will establish the store as a leader or the headquarters for that particular big ticket line of goods. Only large volume departments, such as central air-conditioning, refrigerators, home modernization, and particular lines of automotive goods can adequately support pre-season advertising.

The program must be complete and coordinated. In a pre-season promotion, pricing, advertising, display, and selling guidance are handled in a special bulletin and promotional wrap-up from the headquarter advertising department. This package contains specific selling guidance, special operating procedures, and details of co-op advertising funds available. A selling contest is a popular idea with this kind of promotion.

There are four major considerations a store must face in determining whether a department or line of goods is a good pre-season investment:

1. The department must be a big ticket department with few unit sales but large dollar volume.

2. The department's peak selling season should be a very short one.

3. Co-op advertising should be a possibility.

4. The program should be detailed, with a selling plan. It should be closely supervised by the headquarter office and store management.

A pre-season advertising program will receive little attention unless it is truly a corporate effort with careful and deliberate follow-up at store level. Co-op advertising is needed because most other advertising dollars will have been committed to seasonal advertising programs.

SCHEDULE STRATEGY

Large store or small, discounter or traditional retailer, advertising schedules represent timing strategy, perpetuate satisfactory store inventory turns, and help meet monthly budgeted sales. The retail store must present a good departmental mix to reach its total market potential and, as it is being reached, there must be strategic timing.

The reason there are so many retail ads in a newspaper on one particular day of the week is because it is a good "selling time." A retailer who believes he can steal an earlier day than the traditional day in his area to avoid his competition's ads will probably miss the peak selling day of the week. Schedules must be strategically geared to the selling period—the time when consumers buy certain items—not when the retailer would like to sell certain items.

Given a good merchandising mix and with proper timing, the retailer's next problem to solve is how to reach 60 percent of the homes in his market area. In many markets, one newspaper no longer commands 60 percent home coverage. Therefore, the retailer must strengthen his advertising program by supplementing with other media such as radio, television, and direct mail and/or a second newspaper.

Many retailers do not fully realize that all newspaper subscribers or buyers do not read the paper every day. If an ad runs in a paper with 300,000 circulation which boasts 60 percent home coverage, the ad will not be seen by 60 percent of your market, but probably closer to 30 percent. And of that 30 percent, how many will really notice the ad? What happens if the paper can boast only 25 percent coverage? If it is a two or three-paper town, the retailer should consider using more than one paper. He might also go into the radio and television media, or schedule more ads for more days.

By running an ad on extra days in addition to the usual advertising day, home reader coverage may be increased. However, it must be remembered that all ads are not equally effective on all days. If the major shopping day of the week in an area is Wednesday, Tuesday evening will be a heavily read newspaper, a paper the retailer will want to be in. Through both trial and error and marketing research, the retailer should be able to determine which ads work best on which days.

Markets and newspapers will vary, but all have the characteristic of getting better response for particular ads on particular days. For example, if men read the Monday evening paper more than any other edition during the week, it would be logical to schedule automotive accessory ads, tires, men's suits, sporting goods, etc. for that day. This would be logical, but there is no guarantee that it will work consistently.

Here are some generally accepted guidelines, although adjustments can be made to local consumer patterns and reactions:

- Big ticket items such as appliances and home furnishings should be run primarily on Sunday since these involve major buying decisions by the family.
- Women's fashions should be scheduled either at the very beginning of the week, Sunday or Monday, or at the very end of the week, Friday or Saturday.
- Total store efforts should be promoted in the middle of the week.
- Traffic-generating departments such as housewares, drugs, and domestics should be advertised in the middle or toward the end of the week.

A store will eventually develop ad schedule expertise based on its own unique mix and market that will consistently produce volume, turns, and profits, year after year. The volume of competitions' ads scheduled on a specific day is not the guideline to use. The retailer should not follow the decisions of others, but instead go according to his own sales results.

SCHEDULE CHANGES

Almost immediately after a retailer's ad schedule is released to store staff and department managers, 30 to 90 days in advance of the promotional month, changes begin to appear. Additions, rescheduling, deletions, resizing of ads, and cutting of ads are all normal occurrences. For the large store with many ads scheduled, this could create a very serious communication and control problem. If not handled in an orderly and systematic manner, these changes can become unmanageable and begin to cost the retailer many extra dollars and a drastic reduction in work productivity.

The first problem is to control changes. Are they all necessary? Is there one central point for authorization of changes? An ad change notice authorization should be used to maintain control.

No changes should be made on the advertising schedule without first filling out such an authorization form and then obtaining the advertising manager's or store manager's approval. Department managers do not have the authority to make any changes in the ad schedule, although they may feel they have good reason to request a change. When the authorization form is approved, it is forwarded to the advertising department. At the close of each week, the person responsible will type all of the authorized changes onto a change notice bulletin. The recipients of this change notice update their schedules accordingly.

DISPLAY

The selling strategy of the advertising schedule should be continued on the selling floor. Departmental promotional displays must be scheduled to support the scheduled departmental advertising efforts. If an ad is presenting the good, better, best story of a particular line of goods, so should the displays in the department during that week.

7

Item Merchandising

A store, any size, any type, producing even the very best creative graphics and copy in the world cannot present an effective continuous advertising program until proper attention is placed on the item itself. For the retailer, attention to the item is a mandatory requisite for success. Creative advertising will add to the impact, but item expertise is all-important. Before a pencil is put to an advertising layout, the retailer must know how to merchandise his items to meet anticipated consumer needs. The consumer, after all, buys the item, not assortments.

CLASSIFYING ITEMS

Promotional items can be placed in one of four classifications:

- Basic items offered by the corporate buying office or wholesaler at reduced cost for special-event selling

- Basic items bought at regular cost advertised at reduced prices
- Special purchase, non-basic items
- Basic items at regular cost and at a regularly advertised selling price

Items within each of the four promotional categories will be priced in one of three price ranges:

1. Opening (lower) price range
2. Middle price range
3. Top-of-the-line price range

The selling price for each item will be one of three:

1. Special prices on items the store does not normally carry
2. Regular prices
3. Sale prices

Each item will become one of three parts of an ad:

1. Main feature
2. Sub-feature
3. Traffic-generator

And, each item will have a specific job to do:

1. Produce unit sales
2. Produce dollar volume
3. Produce both

HOW EACH OF THE FOUR ITEM TYPES AFFECTS THE STORE

A special purchase non-basic item not carried in the store's regular inventory adds excitement and newness to the store or department advertising program. However, an over-abundance of special purchases eventually will cause inventory bulges. If ordering of goods is reduced because of this overage, the bread and butter basics will be hurt. Out-of-stocks will appear in basic lines, and many sales will be lost. Instead of improving this situation, cut-backs in buying and advertising worsen it. If it is successful, however, a new non-basic item eventually will become a store basic if its sales warrant it.

A very special group of items provides the power punch of the promotion program. These are the best-selling basics which are offered for a limited time at reduced selling prices. Many stores could not afford the profit drain which markdowns on these items would cause. Therefore, to assure full participation and volume orders, the headquarter buying office of the chains, by means of the promotion fund, can offer the merchandise at reduced cost for a specific event.

The third type of item is a good selling basic not offered to stores at a reduced cost. Usually it is a volume-producing item with a good markup that permits occasional price reduction.

The fourth item also is a basic, but is generally highly seasonal and/or an excellent buy or value at its regular price. It is not offered to the store at a cost reduction, but it is a volume and people-producing item.

In all four item groups, there are items that generate traffic, dollar volume, and profits, or a combination of two or all three.

The advertising manager must be alert to the mix that is being used in each specific advertisement. If a department manager can sell an $8.88 drill every day of every week, it is not a good reason to promote the drill continually. Even if the markup were at 34 percent, it still would not be a good idea. What the department manager would be doing is slowly but surely reducing his market. The consumer who wants a better drill will no longer look to that store. Conversely, persistent promotion of top-of-the-line merchandise eventually will cut the low-end buyers from the market. For example, if a store constantly pushes a $300 washer, it will lose the $150 to $200 buyer who will assume that the store does not even carry the low-end product.

Again, to realize the full market potential, there must be a "mix." The store must have its departmental mix, the departments must have their ad mix, and the ads must have their item mix.

LIQUIDATING ITEM MISTAKES

Retailers should spend very few advertising dollars to liquidate item mistakes, yet every retailer, even the best of them, makes purchasing errors. The cost of liquidating serious errors should be covered in planned, progressive, permanent markdowns. There are times when the "magic" selling price is never reached, and the item is eventually marked down to nothing and given to a charitable institution. But this is an extreme example. It is better to adhere to a progressive markdown schedule. With such a schedule, the markdowns don't become a disaster for one month's budget, but rather are controlled and spread across several months.

If there are several item mistakes throughout many departments, the retailer might use them to make a very productive clearance ad and promotional event, providing, again, that progressive markdowns have been taken over at least a three-month period. For the clearance ad, promotional markdowns (temporary) also are productive.

NEW SALES OPPORTUNITIES
THROUGH ADVERTISING

Today, fewer lines and smaller numbers of specific items within each line are producing a higher percentage of business. For this reason, line analysis (to determine which products in a merchandise line generate the bulk of sales) is a wise investment of time. It is the only means for the department manager to learn where he can expect the bulk of his sales. He must know which items to put an emphasis on. With a line analysis, he also may discover a "sleeper" item—one that contributes a high number of unit sales without much effort in advertising and promotion. With advertising, a sleeper item will do that much better and contribute extra sales to the department.

Another source of increased volume is identifying a below-norm department, a department that does not measure up to total store performance or similar departments in the chain or industry. This department needs attention. Its discovery is made by review of a ranking report of like departments within a chain, a percentage of increase in sales growth compared to other departments, or any one of many measurements that clearly illustrate that the department is not keeping up with the store.

The below-norm department should receive considerable attention and help from the advertising manager. A complete anlaysis should be made of the department, with lines and items reviewed, sales per square foot compared to "like" departments in the chain or the industry, and pricing, markdowns, inventory, rhythm in ordering, and stock of basics reviewed.

Once the problems have been discovered and identified, an advertising campaign should be created for the department. A target sales figure should be arrived at, the schedule written, and expenditures allotted to the target sales figures. The "target" percentage of increase is generally very high, 'but due to the fact that the department is under-developed, such increases are usually met. The advertising schedule should be written in detail for a three-month or preferably a six-month period. The performance of the special campaign for the below-norm department should be watched on a daily basis.

Measuring Yardsticks

Yardsticks are extremely important to a retailer. He will want to know: What are the average sales transactions for specific departments in each of the six-month periods? What is the average markup on receipts for "X" department? What are the average markdowns for specific months? What are the average prices? What is the national and/or regional balance of sales by lines? Nationally, what are top volume, best profit, and top transaction departments for each month?

The above yardsticks, applied to the local department, shed light on new sales and profit opportunities. For example, if, in comparing a domestics department to "like" stores, the department ranks 18th in transactions while other domestics departments rank second, your department is unquestionably not performing to its full capabilities. The department must be studied carefully to determine the merchandising cause for this; then an advertising program should be developed to improve its ranking.

HOW MUCH SHOULD AN ITEM PRODUCE IN SALES?

In retailing, every item advertised must pay its own way. There are many methods for measuring this. The quickest and most effective way is as follows. If an ad for the domestics department costs $80 and the desired advertising ratio is two percent, divide the two percent into the $80 to arrive at the required volume:

$$\frac{4000}{.02 \overline{)\ 80.00}}$$

The ad should gross $4000.

The ratio, depending on store management's objective, will usually vary from two to five percent. But whatever the department ratio, the amount of business the item must do to pay its way can be quickly determined.

However, a review of item performance is not enough. Store management also should look at the total departmental sales performances. If a department is realizing a 13 percent increase and specific advertised items are running a ten percent advertising ratio yet the total department ad percentage is slated at only 2.5 percent, the advertising expenditure should not be cut.

In this example of a 13 percent sales increase, one of several things may have happened. One possibility is that consumers reacted to the ad in large numbers but did not buy the advertised items once they got to the store because the items were low-end merchandise and the better quality items were priced only slightly higher. A markup possibility may exist on the better item. This is one possibility; there are others. Many factors influence the effectiveness of an ad once the customer reaches the store.

CORPORATE FOLLOW-UP AND GUIDANCE

Headquarter buying office involvement should not end with the release of item offerings to the stores. The structure should be designed so that diligent follow-up is maintained. Top level chain management must understand that stores have their individual problems. All store managers do not have merchandising expertise, nor do all have advertising expertise. Guidance in these areas should be supplied by the central chain merchandising and advertising offices.

Promotional offerings ordered by the store should be tabulated and all stores checked to see if they are ordering reasonable quantities to support schedule promotional events. Most chains have guidelines on what percentage a department's sales should be expected from different promotional merchandise each month. This percentage guide is consistently used by the buying departments. If a store department's recommended percentage of promotional goods is 27 percent and it has spent only 12 percent to budgeted sales, the comparison is an additional means for headquarters to bring up the amount of promotional goods ordered in a department. Every department must spend promotional dollars to remain competitive.

The sophisticated and responsible chain has the reports and the structure to execute a tough-minded follow-up system. Good merchandising follow-up is a requisite for aggressive and successful retail promotion. Without order due dates, without deadlines, without mandatory event start and end dates, and without the proper reports to gauge participation, there is little any corporate executive or manager can do to assure success.

8

Measuring Results

Every retailer should learn how to measure accurately his advertising effectiveness. But before assessing any results of advertising, the retailer must understand fully that he is in the business of retailing, not of advertising. Therefore, in looking at his results, he must not use the yardsticks of advertising, but rather those of retailing.

The basic measurement used by retailers is to pre-determine how much business an item or department must produce to pay its own way. This figure is arrived at by dividing the desired advertising ratio into the total cost of the advertisement. If the department spends $400 for advertising on Tuesday and the following three-day sales total $13,000, the effectiveness of the ad (with a three percent advertising ratio) would be considered satisfactory. (The department advertising ratio is covered in Chapter 4.)

COMPARISON REPORTS

For a meaningful comparison, the retailer must create a list of important merchandising elements for the store. The sole pur-

MERCHANDISE COMPARISON REPORT

Month_____

Dept. No.	Net Sales			% Inc. (Dec.)	Closing Inventory			On Order		Old Merchandise	Sales Returns	Goods Received		Markdowns %			Discs. Allow.	Mark Up $'s
	Last Yr.	This Yr.	Budget		At Sell	M.U. %	Budget	Actual	Budget			At Sell	M.U. %	Promotion	Permanent		
TOTAL																		

MERCHANDISE COMPARISON REPORT

This form is by department, for the total store. The same form can be used for the single department with a listing of like departments in other stores. The comparison will clearly indicate areas for improvement. When a department is "par" or better in all of these elements, the retailer can be reasonably assured his advertising investment is productive.

Figure 16

pose of this is to establish norms for comparison. He must know if he is above-norm or below-norm in each of these elements. If the retailer is part of a chain, he can easily obtain comparison figures for ten or 12 of the chain's other stores. The non-chain store will have to look to retail associations or trade information for comparative figures. For both, chain or non-chain store, it is important that the comparison figures be of "like" departments to establish a realistic measurement base.

A sample comparison report form is shown in Figure 16. This form should be completed as soon as possible at the close of each promotional month. Immediacy is extremely important for the correction of any serious negative trends.

Once the report is completed, the retailer can make the comparisons he needs. For any department below the norm in any of the areas listed on the form, he should take immediate action. If a department is consistently above the norm, the retailer can safely say that the department merchandising and advertising efforts are productive.

Important Signals from the Comparison Report

A decision to make a markdown will accelerate sales within the department for a designated time period. But what exactly does the markdown comparison figure tell the retailer? A very high above-norm figure will tell him that the decision was probably influenced by overstocks, damaged goods, decreased sales and/or excessive competition. The following actions should be taken by the retailer:

1. Look for overstocks and promote them before markdowns are required.
2. Check sales and orders of seasonal goods daily or weekly, depending on the size of the overstock condition.
3. Determine whether the markdowns are necessary.
4. Review timing of markdowns. Were they taken early, before the selling peak?

There are other points many retailers will add to this mark-down checklist, but each of the four listed affects decisions on advertising space and each will influence advertising results.

Sales returns are another important factor that flag out specific dangers to a retailer. If returns are higher than the norm, it can mean that goods are being over-sold, prices are too high above competition, or the department is careless in handling merchandise. Each of these problems influences the department manager's advertising decisions and affects advertising strategy and results.

Markup is also important for implementing a successful advertising and sales promotion program. If a department's markup is below the norm, it is very unlikely the department will have the margin necessary for promotional markdowns. The department manager will not and cannot be competitive.

As a communicator, advertising should measure up to some meaningful checklist. The "Impact Meter" illustrated in Figure 17 is such a checklist, designed to dramatize the basic requirements for a good ad.

CORRECTING LINE WEAKNESSES

There are two important sets of facts a department manager must have before he can merchandise his department for maximum sales volume and profit:

- Each of his merchandise line's actual percentage to total department sales
- The norm percentage each line should be contributing to total departmental sales

The first can easily be worked out by the manager from departmental figures. To get the information for the second point, the manager must have a very good knowledge of each line's "norm." He can get these figures from the chain's corporate office trade associations or trade journals.

What the retailer should do is strive to erase any deficiency compared to the "norm." He must know what lines of goods to

ADVERTISEMENT IMPACT METER			
No.	Checklist	Yes	No
1.	Are All Items Wanted Items?	+10	− 8
2.	Are All Items In Stock?	+10	− 6
3.	Have All Items Been Competition Shopped?	+ 7	− 5
4.	Are Price Lines Crossed?	− 5	+ 7
5.	Does The Ad Have a Feature Item	+ 8	− 3
6.	Does The Ad Have a Sub-Feature Item?	+10	− 4
7.	Is The Headline Prominent?	+ 2	− 4
8.	Does The Layout Lead The Eye?	+20	−10
9.	Is Copy Factual, Clear-Cut?	+ 7	− 3
10.	Are All Meaningful Savings Quoted?	+ 3	− 7
11.	Is The Duration of Offer Specified?	+ 4	− 3
12.	Is Store Logo Prominent?	+ 3	− 7
13.	Is Store Address Included?	+ 4	−10
14.	Are Store Hours Included?	+ 3	− 3
15.	Is Ad Extremely Clever?	−10	+ 8
16.	Are Difficult, Cute, or "Cloud Nine" Words Used?	−10	+ 7
17.	Are There Excessive Claims?	−10	+ 3
18.	Is The Ad Honest?	+20	−30
	136 Power Packed 99 Strong 79 Weak		

This chart has been included for one purpose, to demonstrate that a "plus" in ad strength does not equal the same as a "minus" value. If the headline is prominent, it will contribute to the ad to a reasonable point of value, but if it is not prominent, it will hurt the ad's effectiveness considerably more.

Figure 17

give extra attention to in promotion and advertising. He can correct a weak position by reviewing the total sales within the deficient line and asking himself some pertinent questions:

- Are price changes recorded up to the minute?
- Is there evident rhythm in ordering to the selling period?
- Are the top two or three competitors "shopped" regularly?
- Are all items carefully evaluated when additions and deletions to departments' lines are considered?
- Is the line assortment based on consumer needs or on what the department manager wants to sell?
- Are seasonal goods always liquidated before season end?
- Are prices too high or too low?

Retailers must explore every means for development of added sales opportunities and improvement of line performance. It is true that consumers buy by the item, but they do look at assortments. It is a serious error to place the responsibility of producing sales and volume solely on the shoulders of advertising. Time must be spent on developing below-par lines because this is where the real "plus" sales opportunities exist. This is where wise advertising investment will produce the most returns per dollar invested.

Actual counts of all advertised items sold are marked on a tearsheet (the newspaper page with the retailer's ad) and filed in a master tearsheet book. For most retailers the counts will be for a three or four-day period after the ad has run. These counts are of great importance to the department manager, particularly when he is contemplating the next year's advertising and he tries to recall what happened the previous year on certain sale days. This is a good practice undertaken by most retailers. However, the figures recorded can be misleading.

There may be some items that sold in very small quantities, yet they produced many people in the department who were exposed to other goods. How does the retailer measure these traffic-producing items? How can the retailer measure his effort to promote the sale of profit items (generally items that enjoy a high markup)? How can he measure the effort to produce large dollar volume items (big ticket items costing considerable amounts of money)? The retailer must have store traffic, he must sell the profitable items, and he must also have large dollar volume. In short, he must have a "mix."

Then the question comes up, how do you measure a "mix"? The retailer knows he must have a mix in his advertising strategy. The only way he can immediately judge if what he is doing is correct is by the daily cash register totals. An in-depth line analysis will tell him the specifics he needs to know, but the prime advertising yardstick is the cash register. If the department sales are not there, regardless of how well the particular advertised items sold, something is wrong.

THE ADVERTISING CRITIQUE

The advertising critique, executed annually, is intended to keep everyone advertising-alert and advertising-honest. The major goal is to be certain that every department is receiving its rightful share of advertising dollars and that each has a favorable performance of total store sales when compared to departments of other stores.

A critique meeting is usually held with the following reports and subjects on the agenda:

- The advertising reports from this year and the previous year for purposes of determining whether departments are receiving the share of advertising dollars they deserve and that they are working on the proper advertising ratio to sales.
- Co-op advertising analysis to see that there has been participation in corporate programs.
- A tearsheet review of several months' ads to critique the ability of advertising layout and copy to present the chain's merchandising program. Price comparisons also will be reviewed for conformity to corporate policy.

- Newspaper contract review. To be certain that the news-paper advertising contract is up-to-date and provides the best options for the retailer.

- Advertising department review of payroll, office proce-dures, growth anticipation, budget control, unautho-rized carry-over of bills from one month to another, etc.

- A review of corporate policy bulletins to see if they have been of value and whether they have been adhered to.

The critique gives the advertising manager direct corporate acknowledgement and input. It actually involves little in the areas of layout or copywriting; the general concepts of merchandising and promotion are stressed. The critique helps to determine whether advertising dollars are scheduled to departmental sales patterns and peaks and whether each department is receiving as many or more advertising lines or column inches as it did last year.

THE LIFE EXPECTANCY OF AN AD

Every ad a retailer publishes is expected to produce im-mediate traffic and volume. To help reach this objective, a retailer will reduce the regular price of a wanted and timely item to induce the consumer to react immediately, before he spends his dollar elsewhere. With a consumer reaction in large numbers, the price of the ad and the markdowns can be rationalized. For meaningful measurement, the productive and profitable life expectancy of an ad should be limited to three days; four days is stretching. After three or four days, the retailer would be giving markdowns without purpose. Some consumers will respond to an ad two and up to five weeks after an ad has run. These delayed responses are normal, but very few in number. The extension of time for measurement and special markdowns to a 30-day period is without purpose. Any measurement made will not be a true measurement; therefore, it will distort merchandising decisions. Research after the fact by in-ternal or outside sources, although well intended, often is meaning-less to the retailer. The retailer's best research facts are representa-tive of the knowledge of what "will" sell, item by item. All of the answers he must find are right under his own roof. The measurement of three or four days' results tell the retailer whether his item anticipations were very wrong or very right.

REPEATING ADS

Few ads are repeated by the sophisticated retailer. The reason is that repetition of items has already been planned within the schedule. Items may be repeated in the ad schedule, but ads seldom are. The selling peaks of merchandise are usually short and the time and budget available usually do not warrant additional repetition and schedule changes. The campaign moves on as written.

There are exceptions and these exceptions are the spectacularly successful ads that run "as is" until they start to diminish in returns. The moment the trend reverses, the ads are no longer scheduled. Usually these are one-item ads that afford the opportunity for easy control, reorders, and immediate restocking. A vacuum sweeper at just the right time, right quality, and right price would be a typical example. The "repeat" ad is easily measurable and produces best when there are absolutely no changes. The ad must be self-supporting; in other words, it must be able to produce volume to support repetition.

MEASURING RESULTS IN A SLOW ECONOMY

A retailer can never remain stagnant. His sales budgets may be ultra-conservative during slow times, but he must always strive to exceed budgeted expectations. If he fails consistently to meet and/or exceed budget, his turns and transactions will slow down considerably.

In a slow economy and with the additional burden of a market being over-stored, many retailers can very easily and quickly arrive at the brink of disaster. What can the retailer do? How can he measure his efforts? How can he assure himself he is doing the right thing?

One thing he can do is plan well and continue to plan for the long range. But long range planning does not imply long range commitments. For example, pre-prints might be "out" in a slow period. The retailer must liquidate, he must adjust, he must trim his lines and search out new items and sources of supply. Most importantly, he must remain flexible. The smaller the operation, the quicker he can make these adjustments.

The intelligent retailer will not try to outwait the consumer. The retailer is in business to move goods. When items arrive in his inventory, they must be moved out, the quicker the better. He must try to meet the consumer at least half way in a slow economy with increased promotions and the kind of advertising that appeals and communicates with the consumer who is trying very hard to make his own budget stretch.

If a chain realized $300,000 in net sales last year, but this year's sales are plummeting because of the general economic conditions, the company must consider writing new budgets. A profit can be made on $150,000 just as easily as on $300,000, but not with the same rules, not with the same operating dollar budgets. In a slow period, the retailer must roll up his sleeves and carefully adjust to a new start, a new ball game, item by item. If an item is enjoying a 47 percent or 37 percent markup, yet it is collecting dust, the margin may have to be reduced; there must be dollars to reinvest in other items.

Cost of goods sold may be higher, but the margin may still have to be less than the retailer is accustomed to. It may be 27.5 percent instead of 35 percent, but total expenses will also be less and turns increased. Payroll may be cut to 14 percent from 16 percent of sales, but if turnover improves, so will the retailer's sales per employee and his profits.

It is important for the retailer to keep up on important marketing indicators in a changing economy. Shortages are the one area of particular concern. What do they mean to the retailer? Will retailing become a manufacturer's marketing program geared to shortages, or will there be substitute items? Stock-piling the shortage items can result in unwanted inventory.

Lines of goods must be trimmed in a sluggish period and, even for the most experienced retailers, this is not a simple task. If a store's sales are depressed, it does not necessarily mean the elimination of all items that do not meet a predetermined advertising/sales ratio. Like it or not, the retailer will have to trim his lines, but in some categories, he may actually have to broaden them to have what makes a good assortment of basic, bread-and-butter items.

When he has successfully trimmed his lines, the retailer's advertisements will take on a new meaning, a new look of up-to-the-minute offerings. His item mix will be working very hard for him because the consumer's needs are very limited and highly selective in a slow economy. When fast-moving items are discovered, they should be re-ordered and promoted and advertised to the hilt. Keeping up necessary inventories in this situation is the difficult part.

The retailer measures results in a slow economy with the same yardsticks he uses in good times. The "norm" figures may change, but the elements for comparison remain constant. A department which does not have a satisfactory markup on receipts will find it has insufficient margins for promotional markdowns. Good times or bad times, the merchant's final measuring tool is the cash register—the over-all total sales results of each department. If the dollars are not in the cash register, his first reasoning should be that he does not have what the customers want or he hasn't communicated to the consumer properly.

Part II

9

Basics of Graphics

WHAT IS NEEDED

The retailer of any size requires three basic components in his advertising:

1. Consistently good layouts
2. Consistently good selling copy
3. Continuity of image

To achieve these objectives, he must:

1. Establish a set of graphics specifications (specs) and a style for his chain or store
2. Establish copy specifications and copy style

3.   Always properly anticipate and include monthly graphic
needs in the advertising budget

Following these tenets, a retailer can produce and sustain a
very professional advertising image.

The best advertising "look" for a retailer is one that actually
involves very few graphic components. An over-abundance of different typefaces, different pieces of art, and different copy approaches
makes it much more difficult to hold the consumer's attention. Visual simplicity is one of the secrets to advertising success.

The real problem is beginning. Retailers, particularly the
smaller ones, are often very reluctant to budget graphics expenditures. But it is very important for these expenses to be anticipated
because at one time or other every retailer will be in need of the
following components of graphics:

- Special type
- Prints—actual size, blown-up, or reduced
- New art
- Revamped art
- Retouched art
- Special borders, reverses, and other special art effects

Often, many of the above items can be obtained from a local
newspaper at little or no cost, and it is wise for the retailer to take
advantage of this. However, an error common to many retailers,
especially the smaller ones, is making the newspaper the major
source of graphics materials. A newspaper simply cannot supply
everything that is needed.

It must be realized that the advertising budget is not exclusively to cover the cost of running ads or paying for air time.
The budget also should include funds for good graphic design and
the necessary art work. The proportion of the budget allocated for
this purpose varies, depending on the size of the chain and what
materials and services are supplied in-house. Five to seven percent
of the monthly advertising budget is a reasonable proportion al-

though it should include the corporate advertising office's service charge in a large chain.

If a store's advertising budget is $3,000 a month, for example, about $150 should be allocated for graphics. A smaller store or chain with a very small advertising budget and few in-house services would allocate a considerably higher percentage of the advertising dollars for graphics—possibly as high as 12 percent.

COMPONENTS OF GRAPHICS

Figures 18 through 32, which follow, illustrate the basic components of graphics in retail advertising. While some of these are relatively technical and will be handled by professional artists and layout people, the retailer should have an understanding of what goes into making his ads look the way they do.

LOGO AND STORE IMAGE

Unfortunately, most retailers do not realize their advertising image demands an initial expenditure just as much as the physical plant of the store does. The store's ads require a logo (the store's trademark) just as a store building requires a sign. And just as store buildings require design and considerable thought to traffic flow, advertising requires considerable thought to image, a logo, and an easily-read layout design.

Development of the store's or chain's logo is a one-time expense. This "image establishment" expense may be listed separately on the budget or amortized over several months.

The following decisions are involved in establishing an image and creating a corporate logo:

- A "family" of typeface must be decided upon
- Type size and weight for specific areas within ads (features and sub-features, plus specifications for smaller, non-feature items) must be determined
- Approximate space sizes must be determined for the main features in ads, for sub-features, and for other items

Anticipate Consumer Needs

Craw Clarendon Book

Anticipate Consumer Needs

Bodoni Bold

Anticipate Consumer Needs

New Caslon

Anticipate Consumer Needs

Ultra Bodoni Italic

NEWSPAPER TYPE SELECTIONS
The majority of newspapers have a type selection sufficient to meet the needs of all retailers. However what is available to one retailer is available to all. Illustrated are a few of the most popular typefaces. Each newspaper, upon request, will furnish the retailer with a complete specimen proof, or type book, of all typefaces on hand.

Figure 18

Now is the time for all good men to come to the aid of their country.
Now is the time for all good men to come to the aid of their country.
Now is the time for all good men to come to the aid of their country.
Now is the time for all good men to come to the aid of their country.
Now is the time for all good men to come to the aid of their country.
Now is the time for all good men to come to the aid of their country.
Now is the time for all good men to come to the aid of their country.
Now is the time for all good men to come to the aid of their country.
Now is the time for all good men to come to the aid of their country.

Now is the time for all good men to come to the aid of their country.
Now is the time for all good men to come to the aid of their country.
Now is the time for all good men to come to the aid of their country.
Now is the time for all good men to come to the aid of their country.
Now is the time for all good men to come to the aid of their country.
Now is the time for all good men to come to the aid of their country.
Now is the time for all good men to come to the aid of their country.

Now is the time for all good men to come to the aid of their country.
Now is the time for all good men to come to the aid of their country.
Now is the time for all good men to come to the aid of their country.
Now is the time for all good men to come to the aid of their country.
Now is the time for all good men to come to the aid of their country.
Now is the time for all good men to come to the aid of their country.
Now is the time for all good men to come to the aid of their country.

DETERMINATION OF BODY COPY SIZE

Within each ad there are features, sub-features, and smaller traffic-generating or items. If all copy was set in the same size the ad would have difficulty holding the reader's eye. Many retailers solve this problem by using different size type for each unit or section of an ad. Better design can often be achieved by staying with the same point size and controlling the spacing between each line of type. Called leading, this gives the illusion of type being larger. The type set above is in the same point size but using different leading. However, the specifications for a four column by 15-inch ad would not necessarily be the same for a full page ad. The eye does not see things in their true size or the same size under different ad layout circumstances.

Figure 19

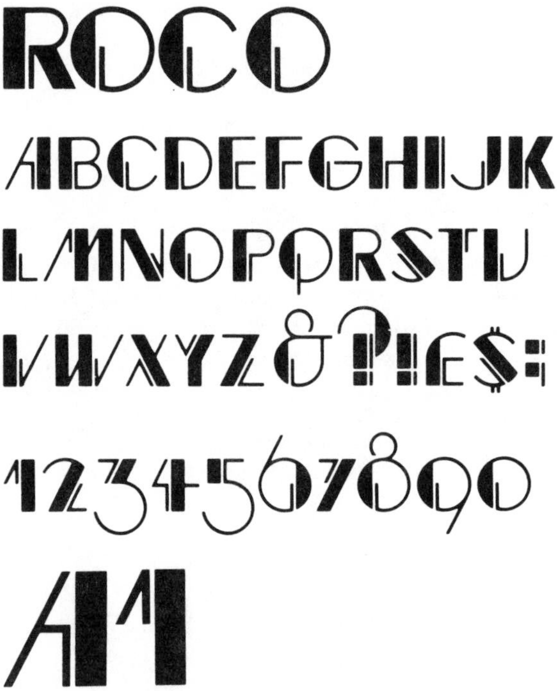

ROCO

ABCDEFGHIJK

LMNOPQRSTU

VWXYZ&?!!€$:

1234567890

AM

DRY TRANSFER TYPE FOR HEADINGS
There are many pressure-sensitive graphic products that afford all graphic designers, large or smaller, the opportunity to achieve sophistication, originality and exclusiveness at a very low cost. The dry-transfer products, which include many typefaces and designs are consistently used by all art studios. The exclusive typefaces available should be of great interest to the small retailer. Usage of the type is normally restricted to display, the headings, or logo of the advertisement. Special borders, types and design-transfer sheets are available at commercial art stores. They come in all sizes in flat or in tape form.

Figure 20

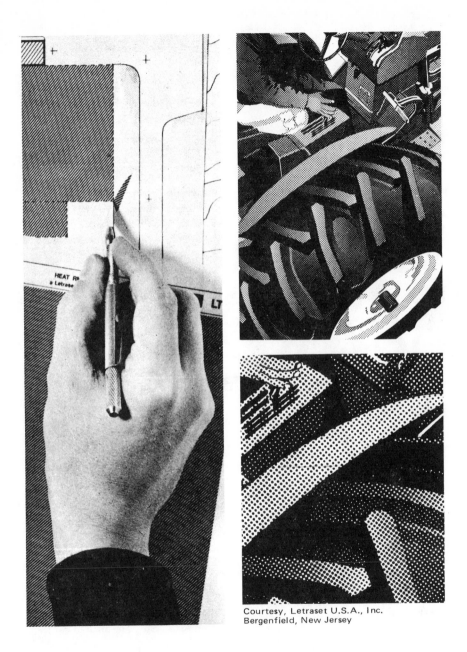

SELF-ADHESIVE SCREENS FOR ART
There is a large range of self-adhesive cut-out shading films available to provide a wide range of patterns for art and design. Used over line art, these can achieve many interesting effects. These films are particularly helpful for brochures and flyers. The films come in sheet form, usually 20 in. by 15 in. or 15 in. by 20 in. and are available at any commercial art supply store.

Figure 21

MACY★S

MACY★S

MACY★S

MACY★S

MACY★S

Courtesy, Macy's
Kansas City, Mo.

LOGO AND AD FORMAT REQUIREMENTS

Once the retailer's ad image and logo are finalized, he should publish a format guide for all of his advertising people. On it, for two-column to eight-column ads, he will specify the specific logo size and number to be used. If he uses rules, the size rule for each ad also will be specified. The logos are printed on slick repro sheets and numbered, corresponding to the format guide. This procedure helps considerably in achieving continuity of image. Placement of the logo and specific usage or restrictions of rules are also given in the format guide, which is very brief and specific. Type guidance for display heading size to ad size is also given.

Figure 22

Advertisers Gothic THIN AGENCY

Advertisers Gothic EXTRA LIGHT AGENCY

Advertisers Gothic LIGHT AGENCY

Advertisers Gothic MEDIUM AGENCY

Advertisers Gothic DEMIBOLD AGENCY

Advertisers Gothic BOLD AGENCY

Advertisers Gothic BLACK AGENCY

Baskerville BOLD AGENCY

Baskerville EXTRA BOLD AGENCY

Baskerville HUNT SPECIAL

Baskerville THICK SPECIAL

Baskerville THICKER SPECIAL

Baskerville THICKEST SPECIAL

A FAMILY OF TYPE FOR CONTINUITY OF IMAGE

The retailer, in determining his ad image, must select a family of type. Type correct for display heading within the advertisement will not always work in other parts of the ad. The same weight of type used throughout the ad will make the ad monotonous. There must be a very select and limited variation of typefaces and weight, but the type should be in the same family and complemented with one or possibly two additional non-family typefaces. Three is usually excessive. In addition, a full line store would not want to use a heavy type face for fashion advertising although a heavy face would be used for hard lines and a medium for home furnishings, for example. Illustrated are examples of two type families. In addition to what is shown here, each family also includes italics.

Figure 23

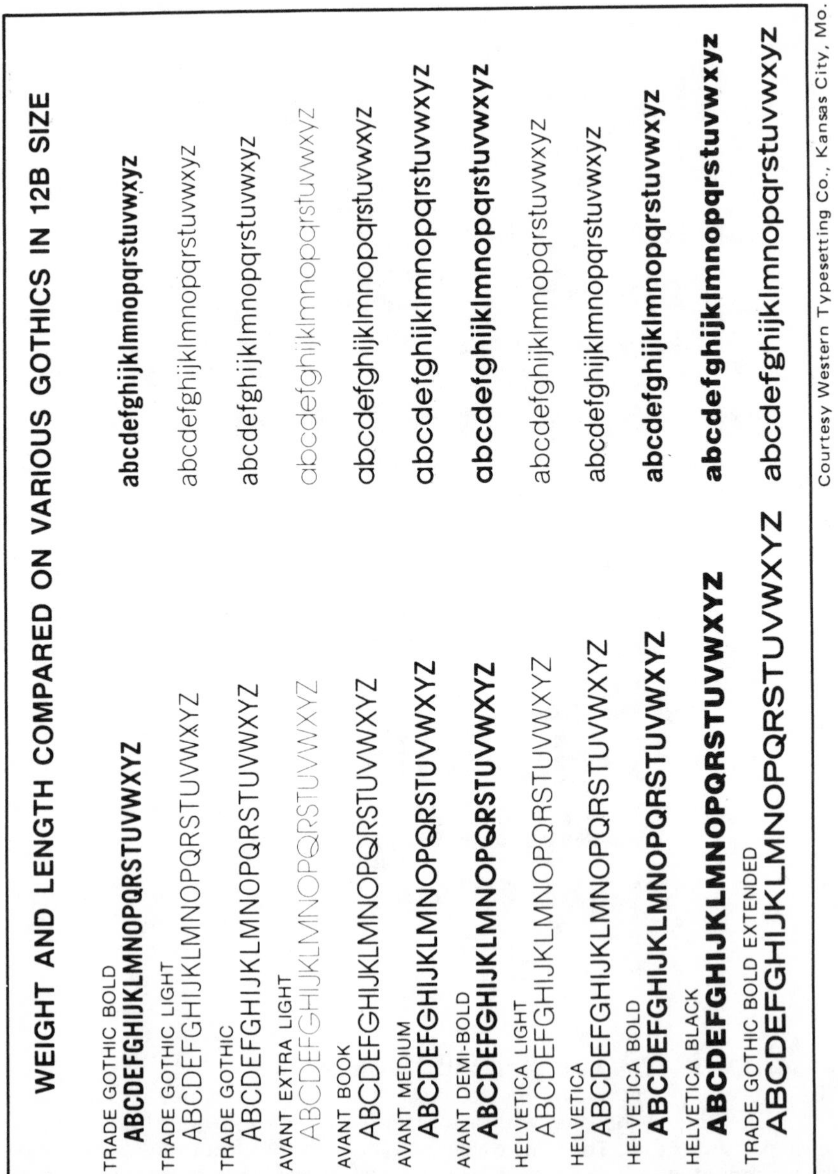

WEIGHT AND LENGTH COMPARED ON VARIOUS GOTHICS IN 12B SIZE

TRADE GOTHIC BOLD
ABCDEFGHIJKLMNOPQRSTUVWXYZ
abcdefghijklmnopqrstuvwxyz

TRADE GOTHIC LIGHT
ABCDEFGHIJKLMNOPQRSTUVWXYZ
abcdefghijklmnopqrstuvwxyz

TRADE GOTHIC
ABCDEFGHIJKLMNOPQRSTUVWXYZ
abcdefghijklmnopqrstuvwxyz

AVANT EXTRA LIGHT
ABCDEFGHIJKLMNOPQRSTUVWXYZ
abcdefghijklmnopqrstuvwxyz

AVANT BOOK
ABCDEFGHIJKLMNOPQRSTUVWXYZ
abcdefghijklmnopqrstuvwxyz

AVANT MEDIUM
ABCDEFGHIJKLMNOPQRSTUVWXYZ
abcdefghijklmnopqrstuvwxyz

AVANT DEMI-BOLD
ABCDEFGHIJKLMNOPQRSTUVWXYZ
abcdefghijklmnopqrstuvwxyz

HELVETICA LIGHT
ABCDEFGHIJKLMNOPQRSTUVWXYZ
abcdefghijklmnopqrstuvwxyz

HELVETICA
ABCDEFGHIJKLMNOPQRSTUVWXYZ
abcdefghijklmnopqrstuvwxyz

HELVETICA BOLD
ABCDEFGHIJKLMNOPQRSTUVWXYZ
abcdefghijklmnopqrstuvwxyz

HELVETICA BLACK
ABCDEFGHIJKLMNOPQRSTUVWXYZ
abcdefghijklmnopqrstuvwxyz

TRADE GOTHIC BOLD EXTENDED
ABCDEFGHIJKLMNOPQRSTUVWXYZ
abcdefghijklmnopqrstuvwxyz

Courtesy Western Typesetting Co., Kansas City, Mo.

SELECTION OF TYPE FOR UNIT SPACES

Unit spaces require a careful selection of type for body copy specifications. An extended type for a small unit will place limitations on the copywriter and cause many problems in design. The retailer, when he is determining his ad image, must keep his copy needs in mind in addition to the overall appearance of the advertisement. An additional three character count for a small unit is very meaningful.

Figure 24

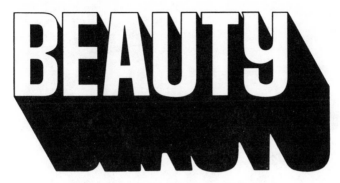

Shadow depth and direction may be shown —
right. left. up or down are possible giving
you another tool to create more dramatic effects.

Perspectives of single words or groups of words
can add dimension and excitement
to what may otherwise be just another bland statement.

Courtesy
Western Typesetting Co.
Kansas City, Mo.

IMAGINATION WITHOUT ART WORK

Every retailer should become familiar with photo composition, cold type. Because of the unlimited usage it affords him and if it is used correctly for the special pieces of art, headings, slogans, maps, etc., that are scheduled to be used again and again, the cost can be justified.

Figure 25

Courtesy Western Typesetting Co.,
Kansas City, Mo.

THE MAGIC OF PHOTO MODIFICATIONS
Any size ad can be precisely reproportioned, in height or width or both, permitting a single paste-up for several different sized ads with no loss of legibility.

Figure 26

PRISMANIA FO2 N 2
PRISMANIA FO2 N 3
PRISMANIA FO2 N 4
PRISMANIA FO2 N 5
PRISMANIA FO2 N 6
PRISMANIA FO2 N 7
PRISMANIA FO2 N 8
PRISMANIA FO2 N 9
PRISMANIA FO2 N 10
PRISMANIA FO2 N 11
PRISMANIA FO2 N 12
PRISMANIA FO2 N 13
PRISMANIA FO2 N 14

Pyramid NL 157 N
Pyramid NM 157 N
Pyramid NB 157 N

Radiant NM 218 N
Radiant ND 218 N
Radiant NB 218 N
Radiant NX 218 N
Radiant NH 218 N

Radiant Cond. NBC 219 N

Romana NA 122 N
Romana NB 122 N
Romana NC 122 N
Romana ND 122 N
Romana NE 122 N
Romana NF 122 N

Schadow NL 145 N
Schadow NM 145 N
Schadow NB 145 N

Syncopation FO3 L N
Syncopation FO3 M N
Syncopation FO3 D N
Syncopation FO3 B N
Syncopation FO3 X N
Syncopation FO3 O N
Syncopation FO3 AS N
Syncopation FO3 BS N
Syncopation FO3 CS N

Times English NL 111 N
Times English NB 111 N
Times English NX 111 N
Times English NBL 111 N

Times Roman NL 110 N
Times Roman NM 110 N
Times Roman NB 110 N
Times Roman NX 110 N
Times Roman NBL 110 N

Times Italic NL 110 N IT
Times Italic NM 110 N IT
Times Italic NB 110 N IT
Times Italic NX 110 N IT
Times Italic NBL 110 N IT

Tribune NL 162 N
Tribune NM 162 N
Tribune NB 162 N
Tribune NX 162 N
Tribune NBL 162 N
Tribune NO 162 N
Tribune NOS 162 N

Univers NA 209 N U45
Univers NB 209 N U55
Univers NC 209 N U65
Univers ND 209 N U75

Vendome NL 127 N
Vendome NM 127 N
Vendome ND 127 N
Vendome NB 127 N
Vendome NX 127 N
Vendome NBL 127 N

Venus Ext. NL 211 N
Venus Ext. NM 211 N
Venus Ext. ND 211 N
Venus Ext. NB 211 N
Venus Ext. NBL 211 N

Weiss Antiqua NL 137 N
Weiss Antiqua NM 137 N
Weiss Antiqua ND 137 N
Weiss Antiqua NB 137 N
Weiss Antiqua NX 137 N
Weiss Antiqua NBL 137 N

Weiss Initials NL 138 N
Weiss Initials NM 138 N
Weiss Initials NB 138 N
Weiss Initials NX 188 N

Whitin NB 147 N
Whitin NBL 147 N
Whitin NU 147 N
Whitin NO 147 N

Windsor NL 126 N
Windsor NM 126 N
Windsor NB 126 N
Windsor NX 126 N
Windsor NO 126 N
Windsor NOS 126 N

Courtesy Western Typesetting Co., Kansas City, Mo.

INNOVATIONS IN TYPE, A HUGE VARIETY

Specify the width or length desired and you receive your type to the exact measurement. Many special typefaces are available today and some will cost more than others. The point is that the retailer has no shortage of means to meet his "special" needs. For the "special" design projects, the retailer should consult a typesetting house or art studio.

Figure 27

Western Typesetting
TOUCHING

Western Typesetting
EXTRA TIGHT

Western Typesetting
TIGHT

Western Typesetting
NORMAL SPACING

Courtesy Western Typesetting Co., Kansas City, Mo.

LETTER SPACING

Letter spacing is important to the retailer for design of his logo or other pieces of art which will be used again and again. The store's logo is in this category and should receive careful review and attention to design. Illustrated is a perfect example of letter spacing of the same type size and the difference of appearance.

Figure 28

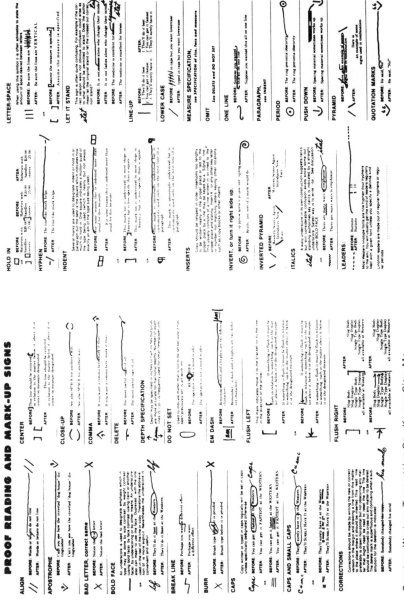

Figure 29

Courtesy Western Typesetting Co., Kansas City, Mo.

RESET

reset **BEFORE:** The defect of this line is of ~~vious~~ — *reset*

AFTER: The defect of this line is obvious

RUN-AROUND

BEFORE: Western can and does take advantage of all sources of supply for new type faces. With machines that cast type from every standard make of matrix, it is our constant effort to make available all faces of type with popular appeal as soon as they reach the trade

1 line 12½
6 lines 7½
balance 10½

AFTER: Western can and does take advantage of all sources of supply for new type faces. With machines that cast type from every standard make of matrix, it is our constant effort to make available all faces of type with popular appeal as soon as they reach the trade

RUN-OVER

frequently

BEFORE: When matter is inserted in copy already set following lines must also be reset although they were satisfactory before the correction. The extent of the reset is indicated by little "brackets."

AFTER: When matter is inserted in copy already set following lines frequently must also be reset although they were satisfactory before the correction. The extent of the reset is indicated by little "brackets."

SET TO FILL,

see *LETTER-SPACE*

SIZE SPECIFICATION,

see *SPECIFICATION of size, face and measure*

SMALL CAPS,

see also *CAPS AND SMALL CAPS*

sm c **BEFORE:** Post Commander John Jones — *sm c*

AFTER: POST COMMANDER John Jones

or

BEFORE: Post Commander John Jones

AFTER: POST COMMANDER John Jones

SPACE

A frequently used symbol. Also use in combination with other symbols such as the delete symbol for take out space

BEFORE: You can see what is wrong here

AFTER: You can see what is wrong here

BEFORE: Perhaps it is for a paste-up and you need cutting space.

AFTER: Perhaps it is for a paste-up

and you need cutting space

SPECIFICATION

Of size, face and measure is usually accomplished by a fraction with the point size and face on top, measure in picas below. Designate Linofilm grids by A, B or C after point size. This is most important where grids overlap. e.g. 12A, 12B and 18B, 18C and 24B, 24C.

BEFORE:
7A Bdi B6
12

A few frequently used abbreviations (strictly Western) follow: S for Spartan, XB for extra bold; Bdi. for Bodoni; U.B. for Ultra Bodoni; Cond. for condensed; etc., etc.

AFTER: A few frequently used abbreviations (strictly Western) follow: S for Spartan; XB for extra bold; Bdi. for Bodoni; U.B. for Ultra Bodoni; Cond. for condensed; etc., etc.

SPELL OUT

A ring around an abbreviation indicates spell it out, but be sure it is obvious what the spelling should be.

BEFORE: Behind Western Typesetting Co equipment stand Western craftsmen.

AFTER: Behind Western Typesetting Company equipment stand Western craftsmen.

STAGGER

BEFORE: They'll do it best You can get it fastest They'll surely have it

AFTER: They'll do it best You can get it fastest They'll surely have it

TRANSPOSE

tr **BEFORE:** The kind best of originality. — *tr*

AFTER: The best kind of originality

WRONG FONT

wf **BEFORE:** Not all wrong fonts are easy to see — *wf*

AFTER: Not all wrong fonts are as easy to see

IDEAL COPY

SIZE

8½ inches wide by 11 inches deep for short takes, complicated matter or matter requiring many marks. 8½ inches wide by 5½ inches deep for long takes of straight matter. The copy board on a linotype machine is small and will not accommodate a sheet larger than 11 inches wide by 5½ inches deep without folding. Whatever the size all sheets should be the same size.

PAPER

Completely opaque, white, of heavy substance, not glossy

POSITION

One side only. Reverse blank. Ample margins on both sides, top and bottom to allow for mark-up.

CHARACTER

Typed in caps and l.c. Caps where caps are desired

SPECIFICATIONS

In the left margin at the beginning of each new face, measure, etc. Use a colored pencil differing from corrections made in copy. Use conventional mark-up signs.

EXTRANEOUS MATERIAL

Do not include material which does not pertain to the work at hand. Do not make operator refer to several sheets to find copy for one page

COMMON ERRORS

1. Body copy typed but display scribbled on dummy

2. Specifications or instructions at bottom of sheet

3. Illegible

4. A purchase order, instructions to engravers, instructions to electrotyper, etc., etc., a dummy, art work, live proof, previous dead proofs, a job ticket, original copy, etc., etc., all returned with an alteration hidden somewhere therein

48 point

abcdefghijklmnopq
rstuvwxyzabcdefghi
123456789012345

60 point

abcdefghijklmn
opqrstuvwxyzab
123456789012

72 point

abcdefghijkl
mnopqrstuv
wxyzabcdefg
1234567890

ENLARGE

1234567890
1234567

HOW TO ACHIEVE ACCURACY ON TYPE MARK-UP

The retailer can improve accuracy in layout by providing his layout people with a master repro or acetate sheet of the chain's basic typeface, set in all the various type sizes. This will be very helpful to the layout artist but, more importantly, it will provide the copywriter with an accurate copy count. Without accuracy to specs, ad image consistency is difficult to achieve.

Figure 30

ONE PIECE OF ART CAN GO A LONG WAY

Illustrated is a very good example of how
money is saved by advance determination of
unit space art needs. Advance planning and
discipline to specs eliminate excessive art
expenditures and, for the chain, gives a space
choice for the large, medium, or small store
advertising budget.

Figure 31

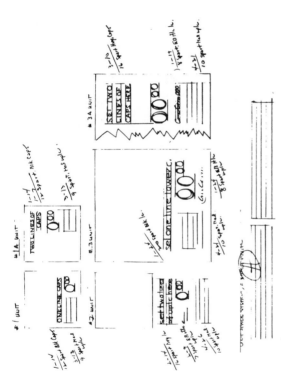

UNIT SPACE SYSTEM, A FINAL VISUAL

After working many days or weeks with his typesetter, the retailer who is developing a unit space system will end up with a "visual" similar to the one shown. From this the typesetter will set dummy units. Adjustments will be made and the end result will be the finalized units. When developing the unit system, the retailer should keep two things in mind, first and most important will be his copywriter. Second, for some units, all items will not lend themselves to a horizontal illustration, so there must be in alternates. Another important point: the units must be accurate in size to replace other units. Two No. 1 units must accurately drop into the space of one No. 2 unit, two No. 2 units into the space of a No. 3 unit, etc. It is not as simple as it appears. Careful checks and tests of size accuracy are mandatory. Allowances must be made for spaces between the smaller units. Note the change of pace of heading type within each unit. The ad must be visualized in its entirety.

Figure 32

- A writing approach and style for advertising copy must be determined

- Information to be included in *all* ads must be decided upon—store hours, locations, etc.

The selection of typeface will be influenced by whether all ads are set at the newspaper or at a typesetting house (a compositor). If set at the newspaper, the choice will be more limited than it will be at a compositor. In either case, the retailer, if he does not have the proper expertise within his own advertising department, should rely on the advice of the typesetting experts at the newspaper or compositor for professional opinions.

The typeface and style decided upon will render a certain "look" to the retailer's ads. This look is part of his overall advertising image and should not be deviated from unless the entire image is to be revamped. In like manner, the art style to be used in ads will be determined with the help of artists and graphics experts either on the retailer's staff or at the newspaper or outside ad agency or art studio. All art work used by the retailer should have a distinctive look and style so that the consumer hardly has to glance at the store's name to know whose ad she is reading.

THE UNIT SPACE SYSTEM

Most retailers could never budget graphic expenditures for the development of an entirely new ad image all at once. The costs would be catastrophic. However, a new image can be accomplished on a gradual basis within realistic budget figures with the help of a unit space system.

The unit space system is a modular system. Various sized units of art work and copy are made up to be used, interchangeably, in different ads. In this way, different components and pieces of art work can be used for different ads.

The unit space system abolishes the need for continuous preparation of copy and art of many previously advertised items. The units, once made up, are filed away for future use and are ready to be "dropped" into any appropriate ad. By building a file of new units, month after month, the retailer will be improving his ad image at a relatively small cost. In about a year, consistently-advertised items will be available for use in almost any ad.

To save time and money, the retailer should establish his own original art file. Original renderings of items to be advertised are extremely important because any creative work can be done with them. This original art will be needed so that units can be made up from it for the retailer's unit space system.

The important point to remember is when you must create new pieces of art, do it once. Without an ongoing art file, the artist will, for example, make a playsuit illustration several times throughout the year. But all he really has to do is do it once and then make prints of it in various sizes for permanent "unit" spaces that meet almost any future size needs.

Determining Unit Space Requirements

Before items can be sized to various space requirements, there should be designated mechanical specifications which must be adhered to. Determination must be made of the ratio of art to copy within each advertisement. Will it be 60–40, 50–50, 40–60, etc? The basic rule for most retailers is a 50–50 ratio of art to copy, but this, of course, can vary.

After this determination is made, the space proportions for units must be decided. For example, units are designed so that two small units can be dropped into the space of one medium unit. Two medium units equal the space designated to the average sub-feature in an ad. Whatever these determinations are, they should be made and adhered to for all future ads or the unit space system will not work.

Any retailer, working with a compositor or newspaper production department, can establish a unit system. The compositor or newspaper will supply the proper specifications for producing the art work and writing the copy to fit. Figure 32 explains the unit system further and illustrates a final "visual."

Once a file and growing backlog of units is built, the ad department can pull from this file a desired unit print or "repro" (reproductions of art or copy on slick paper, ready for printing) for almost any advertised merchandise. All that is required is pasting the units in position and making any up-dates such as price changes. As long as he sticks with the unit system, the retailer will not have to continually prepare new art and copy for every item, although there will always be new items to merchandise and new ad copy to write. The featured item in an ad, for instance, will always have to be written anew. But the back-up items and the illustrations will be all ready and waiting for print in the retailer's unit file.

Converting to the Unit Space System

A retailer with a long-established advertising department desiring to convert to the unit space system will have difficulty setting up the system unless he first organizes it separately from the everyday functions of the advertising department. He should designate one person from each of the advertising department's basic functions —a copywriter, a layout artist, a paste-up artist, a production person —and move them to a location away from the advertising department. These staff people will work on future ads under the unit space system while the rest of the department works on current ads under the old system. As new ads are finished, they are released through the normal procedure to the newspaper or printer. The staff people devising the unit space system eventually will instruct other advertising department people in it so that the department can convert to the system.

Obviously, this luxurious conversion will only be possible if the retailer's advertising department is large enough. However, under any circumstance, it is usually best to train some people, even if it is only one or two, in the new system before the entire staff is exposed to it.

Drawbacks of the Unit Space System

The danger of a unit space system is that it can become self-limiting. This will happen if the retailer allows the advertising department to become so dependent on it that no new creativity will be encouraged. The unit space system saves time and money, but this saving should be redirected into the development of exciting and productive new advertising ideas. Special treatment of featured items, special events, internal communications, and special brochures are a few of the many areas that require creative development.

HOW TO MEASURE AD SPACE

There are two ways to measure newspaper lineage space. One method, by lines, is basically used by national advertisers. The second method, by column inches, is used by most retailers.

There are 14 lines to a newspaper column inch. Ad space is measured by multiplying the number of newspaper columns the ad takes up in width by its depth in inches, and then converting it to lines. For example, a four-column ad by 14 inches deep would become 56 column inches or 784 lines. This method of measurement is consistent with most newspapers, but the number of advertising inches to the column may vary from paper to paper. This is usually specified on the newspaper advertising contract card.

PRE-SET ADS VS. PUBLICATION-SET ADS

Pre-set ads have all body copy and headlines set by the retailer through a compositor. The retailer has the ad pasted up, proofed, and released to the newspaper, ready to be published. Publication set ("pub set") ads are set and put together by the newspaper scheduled to publish the ad. There are four important advantages to using pre-set ads:

1. The retailer has better control of ads
2. Ads can be pre-set far in advance
3. There is usually a larger selection of type at outside type houses as compared to the average newspaper
4. The ads usually require less handling and have fewer corrections because of increased opportunity for advance review

With the cold type system, explained below, type can be set for considerably less money than previously. And, if he is using a unit space system, the retailer can pre-set his full-page ads for as little as $50 to $100 each (a very loose estimate—a great deal depends on the number of items on a page).

It should be remembered that once a unit is set, it never has to be set again. In other words, after six months of pre-setting ads, if the filing system is a good one, an ad may require only half of its units to be newly made up because the other 50 percent can be "picked-up" from the unit system file.

NEWSPAPER PHOTOCOMPOSITION

Type for ads is set either by the "hot type" process or the "cold type" process. Hot type uses metal. Cold type produces type photographically with the use of a computer. Sometimes called photocomposition, cold type is the newer process.

For the retailer, particularly the smaller retailer, cold type offers many advantages. For one thing, the process is very flexible. With photocomposition, line drawings and type can be given special perspectives, letters can be made taller or smaller, wider or narrower. Many attention-getting tricks which formerly required an artist can be accomplished with photocomposition.

Moreover, with the cold type process, the retailer has better control of the total advertisement. Art prints can be positioned almost any way and blocks of copy can be moved to different positions almost at the last moment before the ad is released.

COLOR WORK

While all have the need for it, most retailers believe they do not have the staff or know-how to use color properly in advertising. Yet, color can increase advertising response and sales. At times it would be well worthwhile for the retailer to use it.

How should the medium-sized or smaller retailer approach the use of color? Again, he should rely on experts at the newspaper or at his printer if he does not have the proper experts on his own staff. If they cannot answer his questions, they will know where to go to find the answers. Often, the retailer has only to express his basic ideas and he will be furnished with sufficient samples, specific mechanical requirements, and ample guidance.

Color printing is available at most newspapers and is usually charged on a per-page rate regardless of the size of the ad. This is because the entire page must be run through a color press whether or not color occupies all or part of that page. Reservations for color ads must be made early, as much as a year ahead for very special dates such as Thanksgiving or the day after Christmas. Usually, the newspaper will restrict color usage to a particular section of the newspaper and to specific days of the week, except at the very large metropolitan dailies. Mechanical requirements are also different with color because adjustments and corrections are difficult to make and expensive. For this reason, the layout of a color advertisement must be exact and mechanical specifications adhered to very closely.

ART WORK

For the majority of retailers, art is commissioned on a freelance basis or obtained through an art studio. Few retailers have the advertising payroll to support staff artists.

There are three popular media used by artists—pen and ink line drawings, photography, and wash drawings. The line drawing is usually preferred in retail advertising because of its sharpness in newspaper reproduction and its relative simplicity in printing. Both wash drawings and glossy photographs require a screen print process which is more complex and expensive.

The use of art work in ads is a valuable asset because it can show the customer exactly what she will find at the store. It gives more of a feeling of immediacy, almost as good as having the item right there for the customer to see and touch. Still, many retailers do not adequately utilize art work, thinking it too much of a luxury. However, if line art is used and if the expense is amortized properly, the cost should not be prohibitive.

HOW THE SMALL RETAILER CAN COMPETE

First, nothing can be accomplished, of course, without putting graphic expenditures into the advertising budget. This is the greatest failing of the smaller retailer. If five or even 12 percent of advertising budget is allocated for graphics each month and a unit space system is set up, there will be an improvement in advertising response that should pay for the extra expenditures.

With the increased use of cold type in newspapers and with the many cold typesetting houses now in operation, the smallest retailer can create an advertising image which can stand up to the best of the professionals.

There is no doubt that it is difficult for the small retailer to find quality sources to help him with his "one time" graphic expenditures—development of logo, type selection, and special-event heads. The best means of finding good graphics expertise is to contact the advertising manager of a larger store or the newspaper advertising representative. These people know which free-lance artists and art studios will best serve the retailer's needs.

The main advertising problem of many retailers is attitude. Lacking knowledge of advertising, they sometimes treat it as a necessary evil—a responsibility they would just as soon do without or one they feel is unimportant to the overall success and operation of their business. Unfortunately, nothing could be further from the truth. The seriousness of investing net profit dollars is enough of an inducement to make retailers consider the importance of advertising. It should be clearly understood that advertising affects the total retail operation for better or worse.

10

Advertising Layouts

True layout expertise can only be found in the hands of the professional layout artist. Expertise in layout design is the end result of many years of formal training, education, experience, and talent. However, it is important for everyone concerned with retail advertising to understand how layouts are done and why they are developed the way they are.

FIRST STEP: COMPLETE AD INFORMATION

Layout action begins with the advertising schedule. The schedule serves as notification that a particular department has "X" amount of inches alloted for advertising that month. Attached to the schedule are "ad information" deadlines, the dates copy information for all items to be advertised are to be turned into the advertising department.

The department manager submits this information on an ad copy form, similar to the one illustrated in Figure 33. He will note on the form how much space each item should receive and, for

COPY INFO

Publication Date _____ Newspaper _____

	Ad No. _____

☐ CO-OP

☐ MUST RUN, CANNOT BE DROPPED FROM AD

Co-op Info (Authorization must be attached)

Dept. _____

Buyer:

_____

ITEM _____

STOCK NO. _____ (Mfg. No. _____)

Brand Name _____

☐ DO NOT USE BRAND NAME

Important Selling Points.

_____

_____

_____

Regular Selling Price _____

SALE Selling Price _____

Use comparison checked

_____ Would be

_____ Regularly

_____ Formerly

_____ Originally

☐ FEATURE   ☐ SUB-FEATURE   ☐ TRAFFIC ITEM

Special Requirements and/or Instructions

_____

_____

_____

IMPORTANT, ONE MUST BE CHECKED!!

☐ Glossy Photo Attached ☐ Pick Up, Ran on _____
☐ Repro Slick Attached   ☐ Art info Attached
☐ Original Art Attached ☐ Monthly Art Service _____

Figure 33

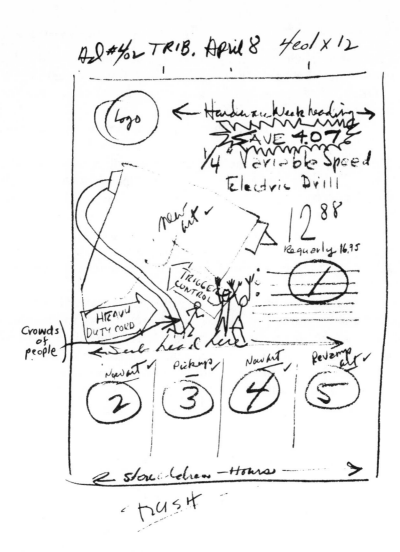

THE THUMBNAIL SKETCH

Shown is a thumbnail created by the copywriter. The ability to draw is not important at this initial stage; what is important are instructions to the layout artist. When making this thumbnail, the copywriter knew the event heading would take approximately three inches of depth and the traffic units at the bottom of the ad three additional inches, leaving six inches for the main feature. This approximation for a visual is mandatory and saves considerable time in initiating the layout. The numbers on the thumbnail correspond to the key on all of the reference materials given to the layout artist. New art or pick-up art is indicated to the layout artist to advise him that he is restricted to the art given unless new art is to be created. The copywriter also has told the layout artist that two features of the drill are to be highlighted and calls for three lines of bullet copy and a subheading to introduce the traffic-generating items.

Figure 34

each item listed, will attach appropriate reference material. This reference material consists of information from the manufacturer on the product, plus actual art work or suggestions of sources for creation of new art.

If the store is a particularly large one, the ad information will be channeled to the copywriter. Otherwise, the advertising department copywriters on the corporate level will handle the writing. One of the first things the copywriter does is make a small thumbnail sketch of the ad similiar to the one illustrated in Figure 34. This sketch is meant to give the layout artist guidance on how much copy there will be and how much space will be needed for headlines. Instructions to the layout artist must be very complete and specific and must include all pieces of art and/or art reference materials.

After a very careful review of materials and after keying all materials to the thumbnail sketch, the merchandise list, and the copy information sheet, the copywriter releases the information to the production manager who in turn releases it to the layout artist. If there was a delay or missed deadline in the ad information process, the production manager will try to pick up the missed time by shortening the deadline for the finished layout.

THE DEVELOPMENT OF THE LAYOUT

Before any layout artist puts a pencil to his layout pad, he must first place himself in the consumer's shoes. He must visualize the ad as the consumer will see it. He also must visualize the ad, not as a separate design entity, but rather in its true environment— within two facing newspaper pages.

The retail advertising layout is not meant to sell goods; its function is to announce. Some store advertising has an over emphasis on the "sell." It tries to make the advertisement a substitute for a salesman and therefore loses many potential readers simply because the reader cannot be held that long.

Basically, the layout has four objectives:

1. To capture attention
2. To hold attention

3. To create a desired reaction (stressing "why" the consumer needs the item and must act now to get it)

4. To increase the percentage of chance for the desired reaction

If the retailer has correctly anticipated consumer needs, has timed his ad properly, has priced the merchandise appropriately, and the layout meets these four objectives, the store should be a busy one.

CAPTURING ATTENTION

The best layout artists are tough-minded individuals. They understand that the consumer has no real loyalty to the store and none must be expected. For every new ad, the consumer's attention must be won.

When a newspaper reader turns a page, he will unconsciously glance to the top right of the two facing pages, then to the left top, all in a matter of three or four seconds. This unconscious movement of the eye must be arrested and held. This is done through the layout which combines an intelligent usage of graphics, headlines, art work, and white (blank) space. The store's logo and the feature item in the ad are the key graphic features in capturing the reader's attention.

When you review the examples of good layout (Figures 35 to 40), keep in mind how your eye is being led. Pay particular attention to the use of rules and white space and how they force your eye in the desired direction. Try *not* to have your eye follow that direction, and you will see how unnatural it is.

Once attention is gained, it is usually short lived, lasting three or four seconds at the most. Yet, attention must be held. The main featured item in the ad must be illustrated interestingly and the information about that item clear and easy to read. If the consumer is interested in that item, chances are good her attention will be held for the remainder of the advertising layout.

What the layout artist must do is get the consumer's eye onto the second feature (sub-feature) item before the consumer either rejects the major item or learns all she wants to know about it.

ROUGHS FOR EXPRESSION OF THE IDEA The way to come up with the idea is to put thoughts on paper, in rough form. It is the only way to record, improve, and finalize the thought. The two roughs illustrated are presented to show that there are ways to advertise "hard to advertise" products, particularly those with legal regulations. Prescriptions is one example. The language in the roughs may not be legally correct for your market; however the words can be easily changed to meet the legal requirements.

Figure 35

This layout presents a good-better-best story, a definite price range that reaches out to all markets. The main feature item represents the greatest buy. The feature item points to the traffic-generating items. The sub-feature is large enough to work on its own to capture the eye. Angle of art, hands pointing, corners pointing, all have a purpose in good layout.

Figure 36

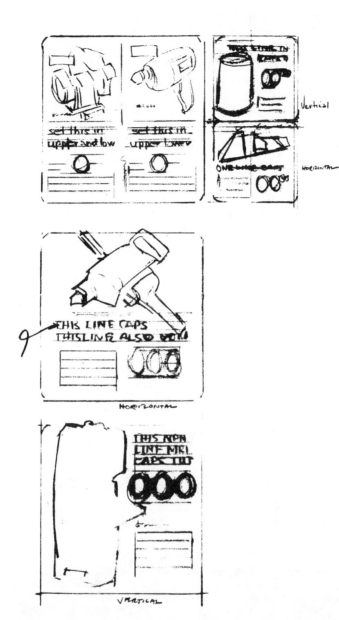

Shown are roughs of a unit space system to solve the problem of one unit fitting into the other. The anticipation must be made that some art, because of item type, must be illustrated horizontally and others vertically. The problem is solved by designing two type layouts. The purpose of our illustration is to show that the retailer does not have to be an artist to anticipate and solve basic ad problems. Once the retailer has a firm fix on the solution, he can work with his typesetter or newspaper for the exact copy counts and finer technical requirements.

Figure 37

FORMAT DEVELOPMENT This rough presents another argument for unit spaces for the general merchandise chain, drug chain or independent store. Again, once something is prepared in a unit space system, it can be used again and again if it has predetermined specifications. The first step is to design the format, then the unit spaces and basic graphics that will work into that format. The rough illustrated could be for a health aids line promotion ad. The change of rules around units adds interest. There is no reason in the world unit space ads have to be overly repetitive or dull.

Figure 38

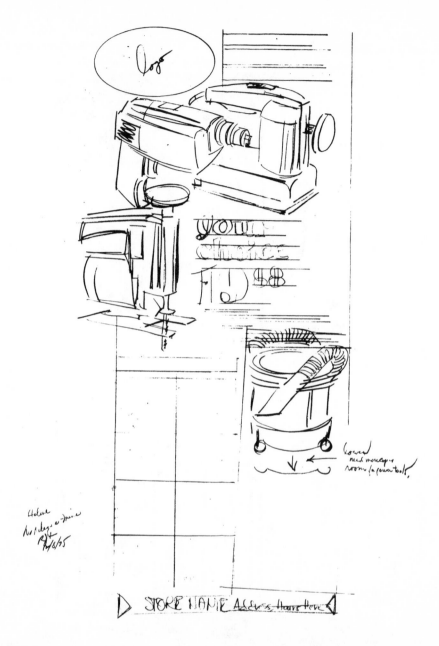

This layout is a very good example of a related item approach. With the power tools, the advertisement of the vacuum is considerably more meaningful and believable as an important need. Here again, the layout illustrated shows how the artist looks at the total ad before the layout is finished. He does not work from top to bottom, he must always visualize the total ad, as the consumer will see it. The feature leads the eye into the sub-feature.

Figure 39

There are exceptions to basic layout rules, the specialty store is one of these exceptions. Specialty store ads can be small but they must be smart, unique, and exude good taste. The layout illustrated is a good example of an ad presenting a perfect feeling of the store type.

Courtesy Newspaper Advertising Bureau, New York, N.Y.

Figure 40

Then, he must get her to look at and be interested in the other items that are included in the ad. By properly leading the eye, the layout artist has increased the store's percentage of sales. This is layout action.

TOOLS REQUIRED FOR LAYOUT

Certain layout equipment and supplies will be needed, and they can be expensive. Some of this basic equipment with approximate prices:

- Tabare (supply case) $55 to $70
- Drawing board, $60 to $95
- Drawing board light, $25 to $45
- T-Square, $4 to $8
- Layout pads, $4 to $6
- Miscellaneous equipment and supplies: rubber cement, thinner, marking pens, triangles, erasers, etc.

For those who can afford it, machines are available which blow up a piece of original art onto a layout pad, allowing the artist to trace and size existing art to exact proportions. This increases the usage of existing art and will lend more impact to ads. The machine costs about $350, but will save at least that much in new art costs each year.

The layout serves as a blueprint for the production department, paste-up artist, copywriter, and the newspaper that is going to print the ad. It lets everyone know exactly where the elements of the ad are to be placed and in what size. For this reason, the larger advertising department will duplicate an original layout in sufficient quantities for distribution to all people concerned. Special large-size duplicating machines will be needed for this and become part of the layout artist's basic equipment. There are many such machines available from commercial copy machine firms and from art supply and blueprint supply companies.

THE ROUGH LAYOUT

The most seasoned layout artist will first do a "rough" of his layout. In some instances, with a difficult ad, the artist may do as many as three or four roughs. The rough layout is a pencil rendering, to actual size, showing the placement of items and copy. What is looked for particularly in the rough is positioning of items for leading the eye throughout the ad from the main feature to sub-feature to other items. By working carefully on the roughs, the layout artist will solve his major space problems well before he does the actual layout.

Typical roughs are illustrated in Figures 35 and 37. Note the reminders the layout artist has written to himself.

Once the rough is acceptable to the artist, he will carefully check it one last time against the thumbnail sketch and copy information given to him, and then begin the final layout.

THE FINAL LAYOUT

Figure 41 is a sample of a keyed layout. This final layout must be exact; there must be guidance for all individuals who are going to use it as a blueprint to create a finished ad. Exact proportions of reduced or blown-up art must be given, along with specific instructions on type size and type face. Proper handling of layout in the early stages will eliminate expensive, time-consuming problems and errors at a later time.

The best way to learn the secrets of good layout is to look at the samples shown in this chapter and at actual examples in any newspaper you pick up. Note how the eye is led throughout the ad. What is it that forces your eye first to the right, then down to the left? This is done by creating an easy flow with a combination of strategically placed graphic elements and the creative use of type and white space.

TYPES OF RETAIL ADS

There are different types of ads, each used to suit different aims and purposes of the retailer. Each type requires its own par-

Illustrated is a typical retail layout, marked up, all type and art keyed, ready for duplication, then distribution to copy, art and production people. The layout illustrated can be classified as a "final" layout, but it is not a comprehensive layout. The retail layout, unlike the layout prepared by national advertisers, does not have to be comprehensive. It does not have to be sold to anyone; therefore its purpose in the advertising department is for instruction. However, it must be exact, and all of the pieces must fit.

Courtesy Townley Metal and Hardware Company Kansas City, Missouri

Figure 41

ticular layout approach because there is a different message or impression that must be conveyed to the consumer.

The Omnibus Ad

This type of ad represents a storewide promotion, with items from many departments in the store. Total store excitement should be stressed in this ad, which is usually multi-page. Omnibus ads must convey the idea that the merchandise shown, although there are many items, is only a sampling of many specials available. (To support this, the store must establish a reputation of offering many unadvertised specials). Prize drawings and special activities at the store will add to the productivity of the omnibus ad, and these should, of course, be played up in the layout.

Omnibus ads have a short productivity duration of one, two, or, at the most, three days. This time urgency must be stressed, both through words and graphics. Also, store hours and locations must be visually emphasized in the layout.

An omnibus ad readership is high and affords the opportunity to capture more new customers than any other type of ad. The occasional omnibus ad event is a statement the consumer understands; she is well aware that the retailer cannot put the total store on sale every week. The layout must be tight, prices clear, and the heading of each item quite specific and easy to read.

The "Supertacular" or Tonnage Ad

This ad is used for large-tonnage impulse items such as a best-selling portable radio at a special, highly promotional price for a limited time only. The layout for the "supertacular" ad must be just that—it does not whisper. It is a bold statement. It says, in essence, "We dare you to pass up this sale price." Copy is not the prime ingredient in this ad; the layout and price are the main elements. Restricted usually to one item, this kind of ad must have graphics that communicate quickly and completely.

Related-Item Ad

Related-item ads group items of different departments together, seasonally or according to similar uses of the items. Small atmosphere art work demonstrating the usage of the merchandise will be beneficial in this ad. A combination ad selling fishing tackle, ice chests, boats, floodlights, camping stoves, and picnic tables would lend itself to a background illustration showing the family on a camp-out. The layout is loose, using a larger amount of white space than usual to establish the proper feeling.

The Department Ad

If it is done correctly to show the depth and breadth of department merchandise, the department ad layout can be an interesting one. The layout should be tight, with a dominant feature and many sub-features which identify lines of goods. Traffic-generating items are restricted to the sub-feature representing the line of goods they are in. For example, a power tool attachment would be within the ad's power tool subsection. Drill bits also would be within that section.

The departmental ad is best run once a season during the department's peak selling period. It should be a promotion, an event of four to ten days. It can begin with a full departmental presentation followed by a tonnage item, and closing with a traffic-generator featuring specials from each of the department's key lines. Extra excitement may be added with a "give-away" from the department. For example, the paint department might give away a paint paddle; the hardware department, a measuring tape. Whatever merchandise is actually included in the ad, the layout must convey depth and variety of merchandise in a relatively small space since the ad is usually no longer than one page.

The department ad, as an exclusive event, cannot be used for every department because of sales volume limitations. Most departments present their major effort within the important storewide event of the month.

Departments that lend themselves particularly well to an exclusive department ad, sales volume permitting, are:

Furniture

Hardware

Automotive Accessories

Central Air-Conditioning and/or Heating

Tires

Toys

Floor Covering

Garden Shop

Women's Coats

Television

Refrigeration

Another possibility is a combination department or group event such as Spring Home Fix-up. The following departments might participate:

Electrical

Plumbing and Heating

Wallpaper

Building Materials

Paint

Hardware

Line Promotion Ad

The line promotion ad is a presentation of good, better, and best items within one line of merchandise. These are most productive when scheduled as a campaign, as a series of three to six ads, starting just before and running into a peak selling period for that particular merchandise. The layouts for these ads are comparatively tight and hard-hitting, with the "best" the dominant feature and sub-features of "better" or "good." Many times the low end is featured and priority reversed.

UNIT SPACES

In Chapter 9, we pointed out that any retailer can develop his own unit space system. Whatever size the units are, they can be developed as a block system with one or more units designed to substitute conveniently the space of another. This provides, in addition to the abolishment of continuous retyping of the same copy and re-doing art work, a great flexibility in layout, for any ad type.

For the chain, unit spaces extend to each store the flexibility of tailoring corporate ads to the store without interrupting the layout design or destroying the corporate ad image. For the independent retailer, the unit-space system allows him to substitute items almost up to the last minute before the ad is released to the newspaper or printer.

11

The Advertising Copy

GUIDELINES

In writing advertising copy, the following guidelines should be adhered to:

- Simplicity
  Reading must be easy. The customer must not be made to "work" through the ad. Abstract and unnecessary words should be eliminated. The copy must be completely understandable to a nine-year-old.

- Integrity
  Copy must be factual and to the point. Every word must be based on truth and fact. Imaginative price comparisons must not be resorted to. Copy must reflect the retailer's feeling of worthiness towards his goods.

- Typography
  The copy and type style must complement the layout.

- Selling Proposition
The main selling point or proposition should be sharp, to the point, and interestingly written.

- Repetition
Important points should be repeated in the copy in different ways.

- Audience
The copy should be written with the individual consumer in mind, not the mass audience. To do this, the copywriter must place himself in the position of the consumer.

Long copy or short? Much depends on the item and the space allotment. In many instances long copy sells better. This does not mean a large ad featuring men's "T" shirts would sell more quantities with more copy. All that has to be said about a "T" shirt can be said in very few words. The prolonged sales pitch with superlative adjectives is not necessary and, in most instances, will not be read.

However, with an item like a stereo set many specifications must be given and a considerable amount of selling done. If there are many features to explain, a checklist comparison box might work well in the ad. All of the important facts must be included to do the proper selling job. The copywriter should assume that any person interested in a stereo will shop and make a comparison of available models. If his is the better buy, the writer must communicate this message to the consumer, not with dreamy copy, but rather with facts and through very careful and deliberate repetition of the exclusive selling points.

THE COPYWRITER'S FUNCTION

When the department manager or buyer receives the monthly ad schedule from the advertising manager, he will circle all of the inches and dates of ad space that belong to his department. Then he will fill out the advertising information sheet and submit it to the advertising department or directly to the copywriter. The copywriter will check the information, and if it is complete, forward it to the production staff of the advertising department for scheduling purposes.

The writer must place before him all pieces of the ad and then make a small thumbnail sketch, indicating the position of each item within the ad. Often, the buyer or another individual will include his own thumbnail of what he thinks the ad should look like.

While the copywriter formulates his thumbnail sketch, he is carefully taking note of the feature and sub-feature items. He is also playing policeman, checking to see if the department manager is following the basic corporate or store policy of advertising wanted items at competitive prices, particularly the featured items. The writer is qualified to suggest an item change because it is he who is most aware of what has been advertised in the past and how. The writer may suggest a replacement item if he thinks it is required.

The writer also looks at the selection from the point of view of layout and consistency. For example, if the ad is for the hardware department and all of the items, with the exception of one, are power tools, he might request that the department manager drop the unrelated item or replace it with a power tool. This will make it much easier for the writer to create copy that has a consistent theme to it.

The writer also looks at the ad information for position of items. Is the correct feature item designated? Often, department managers do not think in terms of advertising. For instance, the department manager designates a $12.95 drill for the feature and a $140 power saw as the sub-feature item. The copywriter immediately realizes, from a graphics and copy point of view, that the ad would be better if the emphasis of space were reversed. The copy and art requirement for each could be more accurately achieved if the saw were the main feature.

What did the copywriter accomplish in his careful review of ad information?

- He avoided a later revision of copy and layout.
- He provided good layout information to the layout artist in his thumbnail sketch, thus reducing the time needed to do the layout and the possibility of revisions.

- He saved additional time by using the correct channel of communication for problems, by contacting the department manager.

- Most important, he improved the chance for the ad to be productive by emphasizing the proper item.

COPY FITTING

By the time the copywriter starts writing, the layout is complete, and one of the copy writer's major responsibilities is to write copy to fit that layout. To do this, three variables must be taken into consideration—the area to be filled, the type size required, and the amount of copy written. When any two of these variables are known, the third can be calculated.

Type is measured in picas and points. Seventy-two points equal one inch, 12 points equal one pica, and six picas equal one inch. In type size,

6-point type yields 12 lines of type per inch

8-point type yields nine lines

10-point type yields seven lines

12-point type yields six lines

14-point type yields five lines.

The easiest way to fit copy is to type the copy with the number of characters in a line that will go in the desired measure. To do this, select the type and count the number of characters in the desired line of copy. This information can be found on a type speciman sheet available from the newspaper, compositor, or advertising department. If the point size is ten point and the character count (counting blank spaces between words) is 21 characters per inch, and the copy block on the layout is three inches, the character count per line would be 63. If the copy block on the layout is one inch deep, the final count indicated would be seven lines of 63 characters.

The copywriter will write ad copy according to the space specifications indicated on the layout. When the copy is written, it must be marked according to the key on the layout. For example, a copy block can be keyed "A" to be in position "A" as indicated on the layout. All elements of the ad, including art, copy, and headlines, are keyed this way with either letters or numbers.

It is important that the copywriter stay within the character count specified on the layout for the copy block. A count variance of two or three characters is allowed, but no more than that or the copy will not fit the space it has been allocated on the layout.

COPY STYLE

There are many approaches to advertising copy. The best copy written is to the point, clear cut, containing all the required facts. Moreover, it is consistently honest. When the copy says this is your best buy at $17.98, it must mean it and support that claim. If the item is the best of the line's good, better, and best and in truth the lower or middle priced merchandise is really the best buy, then the copy and store have not been truthful. If a store consistently pushes its top-of-the-line items for larger markup and implies that the store is giving the best buy, this too is a lie, because the store is asking customers to pay for an item when they could have just as satisfactory an item to meet their needs for considerably less money.

There are many styles of copy and many are effective for each particular store, but if the reader must work to read the ad and determine what the sales proposition or theme of it is, you can bet the copy is ineffective and won't bring customers into the store.

PRICE COMPARISONS

The retailer who believes he can mislead the consumer with fictitious price comparisons is ignorant of advertising integrity and, more often than not, insults the consumer's intelligence. To advertise an $88 washer and have only one or two in stock is obviously unethical and probably actionable. To advertise a $129 washer which is available in sufficient quantity, but then to "trade-up" the customer is good salesmanship.

The first requisite for retailing competence is integrity which often begins and is reflected in the day to day retail price comparisons in ads.

There are four methods of making price comparisons. The best way to grasp the differences among them is to look at some examples.

"Would Be" Comparatives:

SAVE! SAVE! SAVE!
Usual Price would be $6.19!
Special Purchase of First Quality
Men's Fine Cotton
SHIRTS
Just 400 At
This Low Price!
$4.98

Note: The retailer must be prepared to support his "usual price" statement. No dollar amount of savings can be quoted because a true regular price has not been established and no markdown taken. The "would be comparative" is for the special purchase one time buy, the nonbasic item not carried by the store.

"Regularly" Comparatives:

Our Regular Best Selling First Quality
Boy's Denim Rayon Knit
SLACKS
Regularly $4.98 This Sale Only
SAVE $2.00
Just 700
Reduced to
$2.98

Note: This comparison is used for a temporary promotional markdown.

"Formerly" Comparatives:

SAVE AT SMITH'S
A new low price — Reduced $20.00
5 pc. living room suite
Formerly $180
NOW ONLY
$160

Note: This comparative is used when a permanent markdown has been taken. It can be used effectively up to 30 days.

"Originally" Comparatives:

NEW LOW PRICE!
ORIGINALLY PRICED THIS
SEASON AT $10.98
Women's Rayon Knit
BLOUSES
$6.98
Just 500! Priced for . . . .
Immediate Clearance

Note: This comparison is used for a permanent markdown but related to a closeout of an item or line of goods.

It is the responsibility of the advertising department to police ads to conform to ethical price comparisons. Buyers should give the copywriter the first key to good price comparisons in ads by noting on the ad information sheet how the price comparison should be made to the consumer.

Some important items to avoid in price-comparison advertising are:

- Do not use manufacturers' suggested list prices in savings comparisons.
- Do not use "values" unless you can document it.
- Do not use "guarantee" unless that guarantee is a specific one from the manufacturer. It must be reproduced verbatim in the ad and should explain exactly what the guarantee will do.

GOOD COPY WRITING SUGGESTIONS

Once the reader's eye is caught by imaginative layout and graphics, the printed word must hold his interest and lead him through the ad. The main heading and subheadings are used to create initial interest. The words, "Come See, Come Save," for example, are an invitation that is considerably more interesting than "Come and Visit our Store."

Major event headings are extremely important and productive when they are enhanced in the ad with good subheads and supportive copy to give the reader the whole story. The event banner headline, "Jones 76th Anniversary Sale" will die if it is left to hang alone. Additional subheads like "Starts Tomorrow," "Lasts Three Days," "Now in Progress," "Our Greatest Sale Ever," "Hundreds of Items on Sale," "A Sale You Can't Afford to Miss," "Our Buyers Have Made This the Best Sale Ever," "Ends Tomorrow at 5 p.m.," "Hurry!" all help to create excitement and add importance to the event.

In advertising copy about particular items, the heading must tell, very specifically, what the item is and what it will do. This is followed by the price—both the regular and sale price if there is a reduction. The body copy is a statement of facts and specifications about the item. Hard lines copy (for appliances, tools, hardware, etc.) is written sharply and to-the-point, telling what practical advantage the merchandise offers to the consumer. Copy for soft lines (clothing, linen, etc.) has more of a personal appeal to the desires of the customer. The headings for these different types of copy must, of course, be appropriate to the style in which the copy is written.

Store Address and Hours

One incredible mystery is why so many retailers assume every reader of their ads will know exactly where the store is located, how to get there, and what hours the store will be open. This assumption is an expensive error few retailers can afford. Apparently, some retailers believe the inclusion of store address or a map will detract from the ad. But this can hardly be the case if this information helps to move merchandise.

The store hours and location should be a consistent element in every ad, preferably placed in the same part of the ad. If the ad has successfully held the reader's interest, he will be interested in the store's hours and location.

READING PROOFS

One of the copywriter's functions is to check the proofs of the type-set copy he has written. He checks for misprints, misspelling, and other errors. But proofreading is meant for a review, not for rewriting. If the copywriter finds that the copy must be rewritten after it has been set in type, he should consult first with the department and advertising managers.

In large metropolitan newspapers, the proofs are usually cut into sections and pasted on a larger sheet suitable for writing the corrections to the side. In smaller papers or type houses, corrections are all placed on one master proof.

A QUICK COURSE IN WRITING AN AD

It is highly unlikely that any one person will be involved with writing an ad from start to finish. It is usually a team effort. However, any retailer should have a clear idea of what goes into writing an ad. Here, in simplified form, is the process that must be gone through:

1. You must know what will be advertised. There must be a list of items that are to be included in the ad. On the list are the article number (stock number), item description, regular price, sale price and indication of space emphasis, and whether the item is to be a feature, sub-feature, or general traffic-inducing item.

2. You must have some basic selling points about each item and also know where you may obtain illustrations or reference so art may be made. The information may be put on an ad copy info form and references attached to the item list.

3. You will need a layout. Once the layout is completed, art and prints are ordered.

4. You are ready to write the copy, which must be written to the layout copy specifications pertaining to size and

space allocated. If there is no copy count indicated on the copy blocks in the layout then you must figure the count. To do this, you will need the newspaper's type specimen sheet or book. You will select the type to the size indicated on the layout and count the characters per inch. You will measure the copyblock and then know your limitation of characters to go into that space. You will then indicate this count on the layout and begin to write.

Let us assume that all copy and art references have been made available to the writer.

The list of items is as follows:

		Regular	**Sale**	**Emphasis**
09432	19″ color TV	$499.	$388.88	Feature
42162	AM/FM Stereo System	299.	258.88	Sub Feat.
57689	Child's Phono	29.	19.88	Traffic
3201	Portable Radio AM/FM	25.	17.88	Traffic
00932	Blank Cassette Tapes	1.	.49	Traffic

What does this ad say?

The first step in writing is to look at the total ad from the point of view of the consumer, the person who reads your ad.

If it is an ad with very deep price cuts, the savings should be meaningful enough to force a buying decision on the part of the consumer. Stressing the limitation time of an offer increases your chances of making the consumer act. If it is a four day event, the heading may be "SUPERTACULARS—4 DAYS ONLY!" That says it all—be brief, to the point, and always use numerals; do not spell out numbers.

What you have done so far is immediately told the consumer the ad contains super savings, but that they are limited to four days. The reader's eyes will immediately identify the goods illustrated. If there has been some interest in the goods, chances are very good the consumer will read on.

You have a nibble.

The next important item is the copy block heading for the feature item.

What is the outstanding feature? Preferably, it will be what other "like" items do not have. These features are picked out from the copy information submitted and the best one or two feature elements of the item are written into the heading. The heading might read:

Pushbutton—Easy Touch Tuning
19″ Color TV by GB

The next important area is the price area. These requirements are simple. When the savings are meaningful, be certain the regular price is shown next to the advertised sale price. Do not make the reader work in search of the regular price. Show the savings prominently. A favorite spot for location of savings is somewhere on the illustration, in a bold ruled box.

Next is the body copy.

Remember to whom you are writing. Put yourself in the reader's shoes. You might have held the reader this long, but you can be assured he or she will balk at long winded conversation and superlative adjectives. Write to the point.

Completed copy might read:

"This 19-inch diagonal measure picture size TV is the perfect addition for any room. 100% solid state with no tubes to burn out. Touch tuning is quick and precise. A push of the button and the channels are changed instantly. Immediate delivery."

Copy approach for each of the remaining items in the ad is basically the same: put yourself in the reader's shoes; then, make the offer immediate with the heading, sale price, and regular price. Give the specifics a shopper should know in the body copy. To close, use a line such as "Buy Now and Save;" "Delivery Before Christmas!" "Shop and Compare Anywhere!"

Copy is basically a productive means to get the consumer into your store. However, most copy, at least for the retailer, cannot be expected to sell the item, particularly the higher priced item; for that to happen, the consumer must see the item and be sold in the store. The objective of good copy is to move the consumer into action and provoke his interest.

CREATIVE HEADLINES AND COPY LINES

If the item is the right item, at the right price, and being promoted at the right time, good copy will bring customers into the store. With creative copy, more traffic will be generated.

Examples of some creative headings and copy lines are listed below:

"Down, Down, Down go prices"

"Pants, Pants, Pants! Run to Jones Today!"

"Prices chopped to the doors"

"Come See. Come Save!"

"Our Errors are Your Gain"

"Out with the Old"

"Leadership in Prints"

"The Unmentionables"

"There's No Sale Like Jones Sale"

"Be Quick to Save"

"Who's Who in Prints"

"Lift your Spirits"

"He who hesitates will pay more"

"Early Birds Have a Wider Selection"

"Let It Snow with Snowgrips"

"Our Slips are Showing"

"A Sale You Cannot Afford to Miss"

A good creative copy line or headline adds some zip to the ad—a little magical humor to capture more attention.

12

The Paste-Up

The paste-up is a very important part of the advertising process. It involves the pasting down, on heavy white illustration board, all of the advertising elements—type, art, borders, etc. These are pasted down according to the specifications on the layout. The paste-up is also referred to as a "mechanical" or a "keyline."

STEPS IN PASTE-UP

When the layout is completed, it is forwarded to the production department for checking and assemblage of all elements of the ad which will be needed to do a final paste-up. To put the ad together in final ready-for-printer form, the paste-up artist will need all of the pieces which may include any or all of the following:

- New art work
- Revamped art work

- Prints (glossies, blown-up or reduced to size)
- Heading type
- Reverses (white type on black background) or other special type
- Body copy type

When all of these elements have been completed and submitted to the person responsible in the production or advertising department, they are forwarded, with the layout, to the artist.

The paste-up artist will begin by making a blue-penciled guide of the layout on illustration board. Here is where the accuracy of the layout is all-important, because this blue drawing (called a keyline) will form the basis for the placement of all the elements in the advertisement, including the store logo, any special borders or rules, headlines, copy, art work, and prints.

The paste-up artist is usually the person responsible for having art work and photos sized to fit the space alloted for them. He or she also must be certain that the copy, which often is the last element to reach the artist, will fit the space alloted for it. The seasoned paste-up artist anticipates any problems and leaves enough extra space for adjustments if necessary.

The paste-up artist literally "pastes up" the advertisement. He puts prints and/or art work in their positions and pastes in headlines and copy. The copy he uses for the paste-up is on a "repro" which is a proof of type on a hard, slick paper suitable for reproduction.

Obviously, paste-up requires very careful work. The secret is in completely accurate mechanical specifications and measurements. Sometimes, an advertisement will be slotted for more than one newspaper or for a newspaper plus a printed circular. In this case, the paste-up artist might have to adjust margins and borders to fit the alloted space.

When the paste-up is completed, a tissue is layed over it on which any final corrections can be noted. When all corrections have been handled, the pasted-up board is ready for printing, but will probably be checked once more by a production manager or the advertising manager, depending on the size of the advertising staff.

The pasted-up board will be sent to the newspaper or printer. A proof will be returned for corrections; after these are made, the ad will appear in printed form ready for the consumer.

SECRETS TO ELIMINATING PASTE-UP FRUSTRATIONS

The pressures of a retail advertising department are many. Sometimes, sloppy or incomplete mechanical specifications and other necessary information are communicated from one person to another. But any such sloppiness will eventually show up on the paste-up artist's drawing board where all the elements of the ad are pulled together and hence all mistakes are compounded. The wise paste-up artist anticipates some of these problems and develops the following:

- A complete and accurate list of mechanical size requirements for all newspapers the retailer advertises in and for all printers who do store circulars and other advertising pieces
- A procedure for immediate return of his paste-up boards from those who are checking it
- An adequate supply of proper equipment

The paste-up artist must remember that clean work will avoid considerable revisions. The camera sees all; it will pick up and reproduce any extra piece of dust or pencil mark that is accidentally on the paste-up.

One of the common areas of frustration is the ordering of type for headings. The written copy required for ordering special type, particularly reverses (white letters on black), is often forgotten. This can be corrected by always considering special headings as art rather than copy. Once the layout is received, all such headings should be boldly circled in red on the layout and marked "art." This provides the paste-up artist or production staff with a check system for ordering any special type needed.

SIZING ART FOR PRINTS

All original art will have to be made into prints for final reproduction. Their final size is determined by the layout, but correct sizing of the art is the responsibility of the paste-up artist. It is very important because over- or under-sizing can create paste-up problems.

The reduction or blow-up of art for the desired finished print is given by percentage. This is done by using a percentage reduction chart or wheel, available through most art stores. The wheel converts both the original size measurement of the art and the desired new size into the correct percentage for reduction or blow-up. Careful sizing eliminates the need for revisions and re-ordering of prints.

Part III

13

The Job Progress and Production Schedules

Both a small and large chain will have, in some form, a master list of advertising projects to be carried out and their tentative completion dates. The advertising department that consistently misses deadlines or waits for the very last minute is a department that obviously is not functioning well. Errors will be numerous, overtime abundant, and excuses the daily topic of discussion. Moreover, as the operation grows, the more frequently the weak advertising department will fail to meet the schedule. The retailer can help solve this common problem with a follow-up system in the form of a job progress schedule.

A MANAGEMENT TOOL

The job progress schedule is not a production schedule; rather, it is a management tool, a follow-up system which is extremely helpful to those retailers with many simultaneous projects being worked on by the advertising department. For the smaller

JOB REQUISITION

JOB TITLE: _____

JOB NO. _____

JOB DESCRIPTION:

_____
_____
_____
_____
_____
_____
_____
_____
_____
_____
_____
_____

SHIP DATE _____

Needs	Due Dates
☐ LAYOUT	____
☐ COPY	____
☐ ART	____
☐ PHOTOGRAPHY	____
☐ TYPE	____
☐ KEYLINE	____
☐ PRINTING	____
☐ P.U. ART	____
☐ ENGRAVING	____
☐ MATS/REPROS	____
☐ DISTRIBUTION	____
☐ REVAMP ART	____
☐ PUB SET	____

JOB SUPERVISED BY: _____

JOB REQUESTED BY: _____ **DATE** _____

ADV/SALES PROMOTION MANAGER APPROVAL:

_____ **DATE** _____

SPECIAL COSTS _____ **APPROVED BY** _____

SERVICES PURCHASED

Description	Purchase Order No.	Cost

OUTSIDE SERVICES and TIME
☐ LAYOUT _____
☐ ART _____
☐ CREATIVE _____

Figure 42

retailer, the schedule may consist of simply organizing his list of projects on one single sheet; the larger retailer will have a more complex scheduling job.

The work progress schedule does not list all of the production schedule due dates. Only the major parts of the production schedule are listed. The schedule does list all jobs or projects to be done, whether large or small, and fixes individual responsibilities for each phase of the production. This is achieved by requiring the initiator of each project to fill out a project requisition form, similar to the one illustrated in Figure 42. Every job will have its mechanical and graphic needs; all of these needs can be anticipated before the job is begun. The requisition form is a checklist which anticipates and indicates all of the specific needs for the job. It provides the accounting office with a job number to which costs are assigned. This cost record will be valuable to the retailer for purposes of budget control and future planning.

The requisition must be approved by the advertising or store manager. Once it is approved, the production schedule of due dates is determined by the production or advertising manager. All information is attached to the job requisition and forwarded to the individual who will create a job envelope. The key production schedule dates are printed, large and bold, on the front of the envelope. At the same time, the job is added to the "master" job progress schedule and the important production deadline dates for purposes of follow-up are indicated.

All projects to be produced by the advertising department should be included in the progress schedule. No job is too small or too large to be included. Small jobs, for many of the larger retailers, are likely to be pushed off and delayed. With the job progress schedule, if a job is not on the schedule it is regarded as non-existent, and if it is on the schedule, it must be accounted for. Each retailer should design a work progress schedule to his individual needs.

Meeting Deadlines

As projects are added to the "master" schedule each week, the schedule is then duplicated and distributed to all individuals in the advertising department. Jobs completed are so indicated, as are missed deadlines. Completed deadline dates are blacked out on the schedule. No page is dropped from the schedule until all jobs on that page have been completed. A typical work progress schedule may consist of anywhere from one to 20 pages. The person responsible for the schedule will bring it up to date by checking with the individuals concerned for the *receipt* of each phase of each project.

In retail advertising, it is very important that each individual meet his deadline. When the layout artist meets his deadline, the copywriter is more likely to meet his copy due date. If a copywriter receives the layout five days late, it will be unreasonable to expect him to meet his scheduled copy deadline. With a progress schedule, failure to meet deadlines is pinpointed. Although the failure may be justifiable, the problem has a better chance of being resolved when it is known exactly where the breakdown occurred.

The individual responsible for weekly updating of the master schedule should not go to the layout artist and ask whether the layout is complete. Instead, he will ask the next person in line, the *recipient* of the completed layout. When the copywriter receives the layout, for example, then and only then is it checked as completed. If he or she has not received it, the layout is in fact not "completed." Then, for the record, the layout artist is asked "why." At a weekly staff and work schedule review meeting, the report on the "why" of the missed deadline will be given.

ADVANTAGES OF THE JOB PROGRESS SCHEDULE

In combination with the job requisition, the progress schedule is a means of keeping control of all jobs without an over-abundance of paper turning, memos, and red tape. When jobs are placed on the schedule, they must be accounted for; the schedule serves as a reminder and affords the retailer with a better chance of getting jobs done on time or even early.

A corporate advertising office often requires that all ads for a total month be completed at the same time in order to allow one shipment of the month's total ads to all stores in the field. For a small unit or individual store, the newspaper deadlines on the schedule would be for those ads scheduled within one week. A separate production schedule for each individual or daily ad is a cumbersome waste of time since a store can handle weekly deadlines just as easily.

THE PRODUCTION SCHEDULE

The production schedule specifies due dates for every phase of production for the advertising project. Direct mail letters, posters, newspaper circulars, consumer handouts—whetever the project may be, each has its different phases of production. For example, a direct mail piece would have deadline dates for the following:

- Layout and copy information
- Layout
- Final OK of layout
- Copy
- First revision
- Final OK of copy
- Art
- Type and prints
- Paste-ups
- First proofs
- Revised proofs
- Final proofs
- Job to printer
- From printer
- Mail
- In homes

To determine the deadline dates, the retailer will work back from the final requirement date. For a direct mail piece or circular, it would be the "in-home" date. If he desires the pieces to be in the homes on a specific date, the retailer counts back to the mail date, depending on the class of mail used. To meet the mail date, he will have to determine the number of days needed to prepare the piece for mailing. This will give him the "from printer" date. The printer will have to determine how many days he will need to complete the job and meet his "from printer" deadline. This will give the retailer the "to printer" date—and so on, back through each phase until the first deadline date is determined.

The end result is a production schedule for that specific job which is distributed to all people concerned. Advertising professionals usually will build into the schedule an extra two or three days for a cushion to meet the unexpected.

14

Internal Communications

Good internal communications, from store management to employees and from employees back to management, is very important to implementing an effective advertising and sales promotion program.

THE PROMOTIONAL PACKAGE

In many chains, a complete monthly promotional package is sent from the corporate or central advertising department to outlying stores. It would include at least the following:

- The advertising and sales promotion plans
- Contest information
- Special departmental wrap-up of promotional materials and offerings

- Dummy copies of any pre-printed advertising sections available
- Actual-size layouts of suggested and mandatory ads for the month
- Pre-printed merchandise orders
- List of available promotional merchandise

The store advertising manager and department managers who receive this package will require no further materials to complete their advertising and sales promotion plans. There are no straggling pieces of information to come later. For this to happen, of course, the package has to be complete in every detail. Even before the monthly promotional package is sent, stores receive marketing guidance and reference materials and the six-month promotional calendar.

In addition to sending the promotional package, the chain advertising department may intensify the impact of the corporate advertising program with slide presentations, special meetings, and training conferences to its most important and key outlets.

When you consider all of these many communicative pieces utilized by retailers, all of the various directions they move in, all the planning and shipping schedules needed, and all the people involved, it is difficult to imagine that it can be coordinated under one master advance schedule (see Chapter 3 for information on the advance planning schedule).

"PUTTING IT ALL TOGETHER"

Aside from titles and labels, little will differ in a comparison of one retailer's communication methods and materials with another's. All stores, large or small, chain or independent, must do the same things; the difference is that only a few have "put it all together" into a workable, planned system.

Every retailer has a planning schedule of some type.
Every retailer has planning meetings at some time.

Every retailer has some kind of calendar of events.

Every retailer will coordinate buying with special events.

Every retailer must order goods.

Every retailer must communicate the chain's advertising program to store and departmental staff.

Every retailer will at some time complete and publish his advertising plans and schedules.

Every retailer must have ads prepared.

Every retailer's headquarter buying and merchandising department will at some point send promotional communications to store and/or department managers.

Obviously, there is much to be done before a productive advertisement is published. Long before the publication date arrives, the retailer must plan, schedule, expedite, and communicate; and all actions must be deliberate actions, pointing to specific selling patterns and peaks. The retailer must communicate constantly so he might as well be organized about it.

THE OFFICIAL COMMUNICATOR

One important part of the planning package is a monthly planning book or guide which covers the total company "game" plan for advertising and promotion. Printing the plan in some form makes it more official. The dates, schedules, and timetables included in it will take on much more significance if they reach store level in printed form.

All store departments should be coordinated under the chain's "game" plan even though not all stores will participate in every promotional event or advertising campaign. Departments could and should have promotional events of their own, but these must be strategically scheduled to the total chain promotional strategy. And this takes good communication.

Anything having to do with the promotional month advertising and sales promotion program, department by department, should be included in the planning book. What the plan guide or book accomplishes, in addition to improving overall communication, is the elimination of three major problems:

1. Free-wheeling sales promotion communications from headquarter departments to the store.
3. Non-participation or support of company promotions by headquarter chain departments.
3. Non-participation or support of promotional events by the local store.

The headquarter merchandise office must be held responsible to the advertising department for meeting plan guide requirements and deadlines. When the plan, in "book" form or as a three-page memo, whatever size it may be, is released to stores and department managers, all official headquarter planning and organization for that specific promotional month comes to an end. With its release, the promotional month and plan should enter a period of execution.

The contents of the book are restricted to the specific promotional month. Some of the more important items included would be:

- A general message covering strategy for the month
- Operating message covering personnel scheduling to cover peak promotional periods
- Highlights (major sale opportunities) of the month
- Calendar of promotion events
- General merchandise guidelines and objectives
- Sales contest information
- Deadline schedule
- Advertising schedule (suggested or mandatory)
- Departmental guidance
- Window and/or feature end display schedules
- List of specific departmental promotional items available

Regardless of the size of expenditure made on it, whether three pages or 200, the promotional plan for any given month should be clearly coordinated and presented in black-and-white.

The plan book, in addition to serving as a company communicator, is also the master checklist for headquarter executives. By reviewing the plan, any executive can quickly see the total company program and how every store in the chain should fit into it.

ASKING PEOPLE TO DO THEIR PART

In a retail advertising operation, all departments and individuals must carry their rightful load. They must perform to expectations. This is accomplished by various communication methods, but the most productive is having the entire advertising program completed at one time and delegating responsibilities to all employees simultaneously. The secret is asking them specifically to "do." But this cannot be achieved unless the plan is completely written out with definite projects and deadlines for all to see.

MEANS OF COMMUNICATION

All of the store manager's internal communications should be in printed form. Communication will occur in meetings, but the purpose of meetings is to supplement the printed word—that printed word being the finalized advertising schedule and promotion plan.

To supplement the printed message, meetings can be utilized:

- As demonstrations of importance and top management endorsement
- For purposes of feedback and assurances that everyone understands the program
- To ignite and maintain enthusiasm

The store manager or the advertising manager will follow up with:

- Bulletins
- Letters covering specific subjects
- Flyers (flash announcements)
- Store PA system (before opening hours)
- Contests

The manager might use some of the following communication tools to supplement the corporate promotion and advertising plan:

- Slides or special brochures
- Charts
- Employee skits
- Dinners or breakfasts
- Achievement awards
- Films on various subjects
- Quotas
- Training
- Personal consultations with department managers

Each of these tools affords the manager the opportunity to repeat, repeat, and repeat. He will say the same things over and over again, but in different ways.

CONCLUSION

Internal communications, like basic graphics, systems and methods, and forward planning, are advertising requirements that are constant with all retailers. Regardless of size, type, one store or one of a chain of 700 stores, each retailer must meet the same requirements for advertising effectiveness. If the reader can now agree with this proposition, then there is a question which must be asked. Does retail advertising in truth involve general knowledge and general laws? Would it be meaningful to the retailer's personal enrichment and well-being to approach retail advertising as a science? The conclusion must be the reader's.

Glossary

A basic list of general merchandising and advertising terms, their definitions and explanations.

Ad Info	Information and all references required for preparation of the advertisement. Also called "copy info," "Fact Sheet."
Ad Mix	Strategic timing of the five ad types: omnibus ads, tonnage (single item ads), related item ads, departmental ads, and line promotion ads.
Advertising	Paid announcement.
Advertising Agency	A company that creates and produces advertisements for clients.
Advertising Agency, House	Agency created and owned by the retailer. Seldom handles other accounts.
Advertising Budget	The advance allocation of all dollars for purposes of advertising. Includes media, advertising payroll, production, and graphic costs.
Advertising Department Analysis	A report with major reference to the number of newspaper pages produced per advertising department employee and total

cost per page (including advertising department payroll).

Advertising, Institutional Advertising that does not sell items but rather improves the image of the company.

Advertising Ratio Cost percentage of advertising to net sales.

Advertising Schedule A breakdown of scheduled newspaper space by department. Lists department name or number, publication date, newspaper, size of space for total ad and the amount of column inches within that space allocated to the department. The schedule is released to department managers 30 to 60 days in advance of the promotional month with a request and instructions for merchandising the allocated column inches.

Agate line Measurement of newspaper space. One column wide and 14 agate lines to the column inch.

Allowances and Discounts Reduction of regular selling price for purposes other than promotion. Allowances cover customer complaint adjustments pertaining to damaged goods, shortage or out-of-stocks, non-performance of custom services to contracted specifications. Discounts are employee discounts and other special discounts such as to hospitals, city employees, churches, or quantity discounts to commercial institutions.

Art info Factual information for the preparation of art. May be photo of the item, a sample of the item, or a catalog page illustrating the item.

Availability Media space or time open or available for placement of advertisements. Term is also used in merchandising with reference to reorder ability of an item.

Back to Back Advertisements that immediately follow each other.

Back Order An order for goods held for a future delivery time.

Back-Up Stock Quantity of an item (in addition to quantity on the selling floor) held in the stock-

	room near the selling department and/or in the warehouse.
Better Business Bureau	Organization supported by business to police fraudulent advertising claims and methods.
Basics	The assortment of year-round, in-stock, required goods that make up the department.
Big Tickets	Identification of those items with large dollar price points. Some big ticket departments would be furniture, appliances, TV, carpeting.
Billboards	Outdoor signs
Black-and-White	Term used in reference to advertisement or printed piece without color.
Block of Spots	A specific number (block) of radio or TV commercials scheduled within a restricted number of days. Usually sold at a special package price.
Bleed Trim	Printed pages with no margins. Illustrations are trimmed at edge of page.
Blow up	Enlarge. Generally used with reference to art work when ordering prints.
Bold Face Type	Heavier, thick, type faces usually restricted to headings and sub-headings. Also used for purpose of high-lighting key words within body copy.
Body Copy	The block of copy used to tell facts about the item. Not the heading or sub-heading.
Border	The rule surrounding the advertisement.
Bottom of the Line	Low price point of a line of goods. Low end.
Brand Name	Trademark for an item.
Bread and Butter Item	Items that sell well at the regular price every day.
Breadth and Depth	Variety of assortments and depth of line (good, better, best).
Brochure	A small booklet presenting a special message or program.
Budget	A planned amount of dollar expenditures to anticipated sales.
Bulk Rate Contract	Newspaper contract restricted to commitment of specific amount of total column

inches to be used within a twelve-month period.

Bullet Copy One line copy lines, each covering an outstanding feature of the item. Each line starts with a dot and the type is generally heavier than the body copy block that follows.

Buried Refers to advertisement placed in back of a newspaper or one of its sections or which has many other advertisements surrounding it.

Buying Space (or time) The advance commitment to use a specific amount of space or time for purpose of advertising.

Campaign Strategy embracing all or many media and print for a specific objective to be reached in a restricted period of time.

Carry-over Amount of seasonal goods on hand after season ends.

Center-Spread The center of each newspaper section. Allows printing across gutter (the inside margins of two facing pages). Also referred to as a double truck.

Centralized Advertising When the advertising budgets, advertising schedule, merchandise plan are written and controlled by the corporate office or regional location.

Centralized Buying All orders for goods are centrally controlled. The goods the store will carry and how the items will be presented within the store are also controlled by central buying office.

Chain A group of retail stores located in different markets under one central management.

Classified Advertising Identified listing of goods and services within a special section of the newspaper.

Clearance (a) The legal permission for photo usage, quotations, music for jingles, etc. (b) Sale of overstocks and old merchandise.

Closing Date Deadline for original and complete copy of advertisement to be in media hands to warrant a proof. Most newspapers specify the day and the hour.

Color Overlay When two or more colors are used for an ad or printed piece, a tissue and acetate overlay must be made for each color.

Column Inch A method of measurement for newspaper advertisers. The number of columns wide times the inch depth equals total column inches. Inches can be converted to agate line measurement by multiplying the total column inches by 14. Retailers prefer the column inch measurement due to the large amount of space used.

Combination Plate Halftone (progressive tone) and line art (solid line) in one engraving.

Combination Rate Publishers of two or more newspapers, generally morning and evening, will often give a special reduced rate when advertisements are scheduled, without change, to appear in both papers.

Commercial Radio or TV advertisement.

Composition Setting of type for printing. There are two types of composition, setting type in metal (hot type) and setting type by means of a camera process (cold type).

Contract year Period of time specified in a newspaper contract.

Cooperative Advertising Subsidy for advertising. Cost of advertisement is shared with the retailer by one or all of the following: manufacturer, wholesaler, or utility company. For the chain store, subsidized advertising programs and issuing of credits are created and processed by the central corporate office.

Copy The text of the advertisement.

Copywriter Individual who writes the text of the advertisement. Often creates the original visual (thumbnail sketch) or idea for the advertisement.

Coverage (a) The number of homes a newspaper reaches with subscriptions; (b) The number of listeners within a designated area; (c) Floor coverage—the selling people scheduled for specific times and days; (d) For a merchandise department, the number

	of weeks of estimated sales of on-hand and on-order merchandise.
Cropping	Trimming part of art or print to fit designated space.
Cushion, Advertising	Usually 10 to 15 percent of the total advertising budget held in reserve by the advertising manager. A requirement to meet unforeseen expenditure and excesses over estimated expenses.
Deadline	A mandatory date for the completed advertisement or completion of various phases of its production.
Dealer Imprint	Name and address of local dealers imprinted at bottom of manufacturer's ad, pre-printed circulars, and direct mail pieces.
Dealer Tie In Kits	Promotional helps made available to dealers for purpose of tieing into manufacturer ad or campaign. Often made available through the wholesaler. Kits would include merchandising guidance, display pieces, banners, buttons, advertising reproduction slicks, training materials, etc.
Decentralized Advertising	The local store of a chain has the responsibility for planning, budgeting, and writing its own advertising schedule. Adherence is required to the corporate event name, timing, and a choice of promotional items offered by the corporate buying office.
Demographics	Market characteristics.
Departmental Markup	Also called mark-on. The difference between cost of all goods (including freight) in a department and its selling price.
Direct Mail	Mailing of printed advertisements or messages from the retailer direct to the consumer.
Display	(a) Newspapers display advertising; not classified advertising. Uses art and large display type; (b) Display type—type 14-point size or larger; (c) Store display—presentation of goods, window display, interior display, end fixture display, aisle display.

Double Truck	The center spread pages of each newspaper section.
Downward Slope	A term identifying a serious departmental or store sales decrease trend that suggests degeneration and eventual disaster.
Drive Time	Radio prime time. The morning and late afternoon rush hours.
Dummy	Blank sheets of paper to indicate organization of pages of a booklet, or direct mail piece. Prepared in actual or miniature size. May include a layout with important and identifying captions.
E.O.M.	End of month clearance.
Engraving	A plate reproduced from art work (completed paste-up) for printing.
Event	Internal store reference to a sale that has a designated start date and end. Departmental, group, or storewide.
Fact Sheet	Information for writing of copy. Also called "copy info," "ad info."
Family of Type	Type faces of different weights but related in design.
Feature Item	Dominant item within an ad, usually at top right. Produces large dollar volume or large numbers of people or both.
Final Proof	The proof with final corrections. At some newspapers this may be the second or third proof; others will continue to send proofs as long as there are corrections and until one is marked "FINAL."
Firm Order	A commitment for space or time.
First Revision	Proof with the corrections made from the retailer's first proof of his advertisement.
Fixture	The structure in a store that holds the merchandise. Several fixtures make a bay. The fixtures at each end of the bay are referred to as "end fixtures," "head on's," "feature ends."
Flat Rate	A basic and uniform charge.
Font of Type	One style and one point size of type, including numerals and punctuation marks.
Four-Color Process	Full color. Photo engraving process that calls for a set of plates, one to print all

yellows, another all blues, one for all reds, and the fourth for printing of all blacks.

Free Lancer   Artist, layout artist, or copywriter who operates out of his home or office and offers his services to many stores and/or advertising agencies.

Fringe Time   Radio and TV time availabilities just before or immediately following prime time.

Full Run   Advertisement appearing in all editions and complete circulation of newspaper inclusive of all zones.

Gimmick   An addition to an advertised proposition to induce more or immediate consumer reaction, or both. Give-away, combination offer, bonus, midnight owl sale.

Goods   Merchandise.

Graphics   Art, photography, drawings, type selection, and design for the retail advertisement.

Gross Profit   Monthly net sales less cost of goods (including freight), allowances and discounts, and all markdowns.

Gross Sales   Total sales before deduction of cancellations, refunds, and allowances and discounts.

Gutter   Inside margins of two facing pages. For a double truck the gutter can be used as a part of the total ad.

Hairline Rule   A fine line rule. Rule used by many publications to separate columns.

Halftone   (a) Halftone wash drawing simulating photography. (b) Plate of continuous tone screen, i.e., a photograph. Photograph is taken of wash drawing through a screen on the camera that breaks the picture into small dots.

Hard Lines   Hardware, paint, plumbing and heating, automotive, farm, building, and repair, and similar merchandise.

Hand-Out   A printed, inexpensive sales message piece distributed to store traffic for purpose of highlighting outstanding specials.

Home Coverage   The number of homes subscribing to a

newspaper representing a percentage to total homes in the market.

Insertion Order Order for placement of an ad in a publication. Specifies date of order, publication date, size of ad, ad identification, rate per column inch, total cost, and special instructions or requests for specific location. Individual insertion order accompanies every ad.

Independent A store that is not part of a chain.

Initial Orders First orders placed for goods before the start of a selling season.

Inventory (a) Book—amount of all goods recorded as on hand; (b) Actual or physical—the amount of all goods on hand, including warehouse and stockrooms.

Inventory Overage The difference between the book inventory and the physical inventory when the physical inventory is more.

Inventory Shrinkage The loss of profit through unrecorded markdowns, discounts and allowances, theft, etc.

Inventory Shortage The difference between the book inventory and the actual physical inventory when the physical inventory is less.

Inventory Turnover The speed or times the average inventory is sold and replaced. To find turnover, start with the opening inventory added to all closing inventories, divide the total by total number of inventories added. The answer will be the average inventory. New sales divided by the average inventory will equal the rate of annual turnover.

Item Merchandising The act of concentrating on the single item to anticipated consumer needs for purpose of assuring balance and mix.

Item Mix Low, middle, and top-of-the-line strategically timed to afford the retailer full market potential.

Job Requisition Original job order listing all mechanical requirements, graphic needs, and quantities required plus final ship or completion date.

Keyline Paste-up of the advertisement or printed

piece. All type, art are pasted in position per layout and ready for camera. Also referred to as a mechanical.

Layout
Drawing of the advertisement to actual mechanical requirements of the publication. Purpose is to see how the ad will look and also serve as a blueprint for instruction to the keyline (paste-up) artist, artist, copywriter, production department, and the typesetter.

Leading
The insertion of space between lines of body copy. When leaded, body copy will appear larger.

Line Drawing
A drawing without shading or tone.

Line Promotion Ad
Advertisement including good, better, best-of-a-line of goods. The high price point, middle, and low end.

Lineage
Denotes total lines or column inches of an advertisement or series of advertisements.

Lineage Report
A monthly tabulation of retailer's lineage by category, prepared by the newspaper.

Logo
Store name trademark used in advertisement. Also called logotype.

Loss Leader
A wanted item advertised and sold below the retailer's cost.

Major Event
Departmental or total store effort embracing all aspects of advertising and sales promotion, including the sales contest. Scheduled to major selling peaks, generally one in spring and one in fall, excluding Christmas.

Markdowns
(a) A reduction in selling price to meet a competitor's low price (permanent markdown) or to accelerate the movement of goods for a specific period of time (temporary promotional markdown); (b) A loss of profits.

Markup
The difference between the cost of the item (including freight) and its selling price. Also called mark-on.

Markup Percent
The markup dollars divided by the selling price.

Media	The means by which the retailer communicates with the consumer. Major media are newspaper, radio, and TV.
Merchandise Fund	The chain's centrally controlled cooperative advertising fund.
Merchandising	All other than advertising, display, and personal selling. The work of anticipating basic consumer needs with a calculated mix to assure maximum inventory turns, sales volume, and profits.
Merchandise Office	The office within a store that coordinates and processes the ordering and receiving of orders of goods, maintains stock counting controls, and inventory records by department.
Merchant	One who merchandises to anticipated consumer needs.
Model Ads	Dummy ads, suggested ads, or sample ads released to stores in the field by the corporate advertising or retail sales department.
National Brand	A manufacturer's item distributed nationally through many outlets.
Net Profit	That which remains of the sales price after costs of item, allowances and discounts, markdowns, advertising, display, store operating costs, and all other expenses have been deducted.
Net Sales	Sales of a department or store, less allowances and discounts, returns and cancellations.
On-Order	The amount of goods ordered and committed for.
On-Order File	File kept until the goods are received in the store or warehouse. The file is reviewed weekly and for those items not received but needed, a follow-up notice is mailed to the source.
One-Time Buy	A non-basic item, bought, sold, and not reordered.
On-Hand	Amount of goods owned by the department, including stock rooms and warehouse stocks.

Omnibus Ad	Advertisement that includes representative items from all departments. Traffic-producing ad.
Order Due Date	The deadline promotional item orders are to be at central buying office or source of supply.
Patterns, Sales	Selling peak and valleys of an item, line of goods, department, or store.
Photocomposition	A method of setting type by photography process. Also referred to as "cold type."
Pica	Unit of measurement for width. There are six picas to the inch.
Plate	Engraving (metal) made from art work or photograph for printing.
Point	A measurement of type. Although smaller point sizes are available a retailer will seldom use less than eight point or more than 72 point. (72 points equal one inch)
Pre-Opening Expense	Special account, for purposes of spreading ad expenditure two to seven months, and identification of those necessary advertising expenditures that do not produce immediate sales.
Pre-Print	A circular, usually centrally merchandised and printed. Usually scheduled for newspaper insertion at special low rate.
Preferred Position	Specific location of ad in a newspaper. Available through most newspapers at a premium rate.
Press Date	Day and hour publication press starts to print.
Price Lining	Price arrangement and item line selection to buying habits of customers; i.e. $1.99 may be habit of community—not over $2.00 price point.
Prime Time	The best radio/TV time. For radio, drive time; for TV, generally 7 to 10:30 p.m.
Prints	Screened reproduction of art work, sized to layout.
Private Brand	An item sold exclusively through a store or chain under its own label. Some made to retailer's specifications; private label.

Promotional Item Worksheet	An advance monthly summary of a department's items scheduled to be advertised. Lists for each item date to be in the ad, the event, stock number, item description, regular and selling price, dollar markdown of each and total of markdown dollars, departmental markdown dollar budget, percent of estimated sales of the promotional markdown items to total department sales, estimated unit sales for each item, and the current on-hand on-order quantity for each of the items.
Quota	A department's share of the total store sales objective for a major event and/or individual share of departmental sales objective.
Rain Check	Method of satisfying consumer desire for advertised item not in stock. With the rain check issued to them, the consumers may purchase the item at a later date, when it is in stock, at the original advertised price.
Reorder	The reordering of an item to replace sold stock or increase coverage to an increased unit sales trend.
Report Direct Store	Store that is not in a group, district, or zone. The store reports directly to the corporate home office or a regional office.
Repro Slicks	Sharp printed reproductions of art and type on very white and hard slick paper, suitable to be reproduced as part of the pasted up ad.
Rough Layout	The first step the layout artist takes to indicate sizing and positioning of units to be included in the ad.
Sales Budgets	Estimated sales volume. The basis for all other planned expense.
Sales Promotion	All activities of selling and merchandising other than advertising, basic display, and personal selling.
Sales to Date	Accumulated sales by department or total store for month to date and/or year to date.

Selling Cost, Individual   Total earnings divided by net sales for the same period = selling cost percentage.

Set And Hold   Instruction to newspaper to set and proof an ad but hold for specific running date. A snow shovel would be a candidate for a "set and hold" ad.

Set-to-Fill   Instructions to newspaper to set copy in point size that will fill area designated on the layout.

Special Purchase   A one-time buy. An item, generally seasonal, not included in regular inventory.

Specification Buying   A retail chain contracts with a manufacturer to produce a product to the retailer's specification to be sold under the retailer's own label.

Spot Order   Order of items after a non-scheduled count to avoid out-of-stock condition.

Staple Item   An item that sells well year round. Hosiery and sheets are examples, but all items have their own sales peaks and valleys.

Store Trim   Store decorations, other than major display.

Straight List   A list of items a department will advertise for a month or the items of a specific ad. Lists the stock number, item description, regular price and sale price.

Sub-feature   The second most dominant item within an ad.

Tag Line   The retailer's identification and/or message at the end of the manufacturer's TV or radio spot.

Target Sales Figure   A sales objective in excess of the sales budget.

Tearsheet   Copy of a complete newspaper page containing the retailer's ad.

Timetable, Planning   A listing of required completion times goods are to be in store, advertised, and sold.

Tonnage Ad   Large size single item ad featuring a best selling wanted item at a reduced price for a limited time only.

Trademark   Design that identifies a product.

Traffic Items   Items within an ad, usually requiring a

	small amount of space, that produce large numbers of shoppers.
Trend	Current and accumulated sales for six to eight weeks indicative of a persistent increase or decrease.
Type Page	The area of the newspaper or magazine page which type can occupy.

Index